WRITER'S BASIC BOOKSHELF

How To Write

Write

& SELL

A

COLUMN

Julie Raskin

Carolyn Males

Writer's Digest Books
Cincinnati, Ohio

DEDICATION

To Stanley and Dick,
The pillars—if not the columns—of our lives.

92 91 90 89 88 87   5 4 3 2 1

Library of Congress Cataloging-in-Publication Data
Raskin, Julie, 1941–
  How to write and sell a column.
  Bibliography: p.
  Includes index.
  1. Journalism—Authorship. 2. Newspapers—Sections, columns, etc. I. Males, Carolyn. II. Title.
PN4784.C65R37 1987   808'.06607   87-25251
ISBN 0-89879-295-9

Design by Judy Allan.

The following page constitutes an extension of this copyright page.

CONTENTS

ACKNOWLEDGMENTS

A book like this requires a lot of research and column gathering from publications throughout the United States. To get a wide sampling of columnists, we deputized our friends from across the nation to act as our eyes and to go through their local papers, scouting out their favorites. This roundup brought us a wealth of material that helped set the foundation of this book. For their help we thank Ann Ackerson, Sue Ainsworth, Amy Anderson, Jeanne Archuleta, Kris Blay, Beverly Breton, Terre Brown, Mary Burns, Melvin and Hazel Chernault, Tom Christy, Arlene Cohen, Mary Rose Contey, Steve Dicker, Terri Diener, Theresa and Frank Fackino, Hilda Friedlander, Jo Friedlander, Sid Friedlander, Ron Friedman, Mary Gibson, Walter and Helen Goldstein, Cliff Graubart, Gary Greene, Judy Griswold, Marie and Ed Hacker, Susan Hamble, Ann Hart, Ellis Hughes, Fred Kaplan, Alice Koelle, Marie Lehnert, Alice Leonhardt, Loree Lough, Ruth Males, Mickey Maribo, Lorna Mattern, Jane Moos, Esther and Sidney Nemetz, Ellen Rennels, Carol and John Roberts, Sue Robison, Eddie Rose, Marc Shafir, Jeanne Slack, Doris Starks, Bob and Sally Thigpen, Polly Thornton, Fran Valentine, Gina Venn, Joseph Vogel, and Virginia and Harry Wolf.

Editors and columnists also got roped into this project, and for their willingness to help we thank Paul Barger, *The Winslow Mail*; Chris Conti, San Francisco *Chronicle*; Wayne Ezell, *Boca Raton News*; Doreen Lindahl and Alan Zdon, *The Hibbing Daily Tribune*; Albert J. Pinder, *The Grinnell Herald-Register*; John E. Simonds, *Honolulu Star-Bulletin*; Robert L. Steed, columnist; and Kent Sturgis, *News-Miner* (Fairbanks, Alaska).

To those columnists and editors we rounded up and captured for a goodly amount of their time, we offer special thanks: George "Doc" and Katy Abraham, Michael Argirion, Stephen Atlas, Dave Barry, Gordon Bishop, Art Buchwald, Richard Cohen, Al Counts, Colleen Cowles, Paul Deegan, Anne-Marie DeGeorge, Florence De Santis, Joe Doggett, John

Douglas, Diana L. Drake, Jerry Feigen, Ramsey Flynn, Michael Fox, Barry Garron, Barbara Gibbons, Ruth Glick, Joe Graedon, Richard "Gut" Gutwillig, George C. Hamersley, Dorothy Hammond, Dee Hardie, Betty Lehan Harragan, James Head, Grace Hechinger, Heloise, Cathy Johnson, Bill Kurtzeborn, Mike Levine, Jake Morrissey, George Plagenz, Fred Reed, Isaac Rehert, Tom Reinken, Roger Rosenblatt, Sue Rusche, Bob Russell, Rita St. Clair, Charles Salter, Bonnie J. Schupp, Bob Schwabach, Lew Sichelman, Roger Simon, Martin Sloane, Joseph Spear, Bill Speers, John R. Starr, Jane and Michael Stern, Chef Louis Szathmary, Cheryl Lee Terry, and Vicki Williams.

Special thanks to Jeffrey L. Squires for his help and patience in guiding us through the rugged terrain of syndicate contracts and writers' legal concerns.

We especially thank our editor at Writer's Digest Books, Sharon Rudd, whose guidance was invaluable and patience was much appreciated. Thanks also to Jean M. Fredette, Sheila Freeman, Carol Cartaino, and Kirk Polking at Writer's Digest Books. And thanks, too, to our agent Linda Hayes.

And last, but never least, we thank our ever-patient, tolerant and droll spouses, Stanley and Dick, and also Carolyn's German shepherd, Jake, who kept the mail carrier, UPS delivery drivers, and door-to-door solicitors from interrupting our work.

PREFACE

Each dawn the two of us open our front doors, tromp across our front lawns, and bring in the newspapers. Then, spreading *The Washington Post* out on our kitchen tables, we each grab a glass of juice and turn to Richard Cohen's commentary, Ann Landers's no-nonsense advice, and Jonathan Yardley's musings on books and other subjects. With her morning dose of comic strips, Julie includes Alfred Sheinwold's bridge column. Then, glancing up the page, she checks the day's horoscopes. Carolyn goes in for the heavy stuff. She relies on the op-ed page along with the news to see what's going on in the world.

In the rest of our periodical reading, we also indulge our penchant for columns. Every month Julie scans the listings and descriptions of new compositions and arrangements in *The Instrumentalist* looking for pieces her community concert band might play. When Carolyn flips through *Photographic* magazine each month she finds that Bill Hunter's question-and-answer column fills her in on the newest camera equipment and latest photographic techniques.

Readers like us get hooked on columns. Think about how many of us devoured investigative reporter Jack Anderson's words during the Watergate scandal. Or how many pairs of eyes look to "Dear Abby" for words of wisdom or real-life soap opera each day. Without a daily ration of columnists, a morning doesn't get off to the right start—it's sort of like trying to get going without a wake-me-up cup of coffee or tea.

Over the years, we have wondered what makes people turn to the same columnists day in and day out. So we asked around:

> *"I enjoy getting to know a person through his or her column. It can get to be an immensely satisfying, if one-sided, 'relationship.' I like following other people's arguments and logic and carrying on a dialogue with them in my head."*—Amy Anderson, program specialist for a housing agency.

"It seems to me that a good column must have a decent subject, a strong opinion and a modicum of accuracy. It isn't necessary for me to agree with the writer. In fact, if I know anything about the subject, I'll probably disagree with anything anybody writes on it. It's part of my heritage."—Sid Friedlander, former assistant sports editor of the New York Post.

"I read columns for the usual, general reasons: a focusing of the news, an interpretation of events, a human voice crying out from the well of cold hard facts and figures—also, just to come across some excellent writing now and then. Columnists have plenty of off-days, like the rest of us, but then suddenly on a rainy Tuesday morning one will be right on the mark, reading like Shakespeare."—Steve Dicker, U.S. postal worker.

"I feel I know them [my favorite columnists]—that if I ran into them on the street, they'd smile and say 'hi.' Let's face it, these folks bare their souls to us—daily, weekly— the most intimate corners of their minds are exposed and vulnerable. . . ."—Terre Brown, freelance writer.

Familiarity. Stimulation. Entertainment. Information. They're what keep readers coming back for more. Some columnoholics crave the intimacy that comes from a long acquaintance with a writer's voice. Think about how many of us consider Andy Rooney a pal after taking in his bemused explanations of the intricacies of modern life via his newspaper commentary and electronic column on *60 Minutes*.

Readers delight in getting their information or opinions spiced with clever comments, salted with a soupçon of sarcasm, and sharpened with a twist of witty wordplay. A fine turn of phrase, a vivid picture, a captivating delivery—these ingredients mixed with a logical presentation of ideas and first-class reasoning form a well-balanced base. Add that to a subject that readers can identify with or one that has relevance to their lives, and you have a recipe for a column that audiences will gobble up.

INTRODUCTION

As writers, writing teachers, and avid column readers, we have long wondered how columnists learn to be columnists, how they manage to cram their thoughts into 800-word chunks, replenish their bank of ideas, and convince an editor that their voice should be heard.

Since we couldn't find any books on how to write a column, we decided to pen one. For the past year we have collected columns and interviewed readers and writers about column writing so we could write this guide.

We have divided the book into seven chapters that will show you how to come up with a saleable idea, choose a format, make a point in a few well-chosen words, market your column, promote your work, and self-syndicate the column or approach a syndicate. We'll explore ways to get your words pored over and your opinions pondered—and to claim your own special corner of a newspaper, magazine, or newsletter page. Interspersed with the information are practical exercises to do and points to consider.

This book is intended as a guide to column writing, not as an introductory writing text. To learn the fundamentals, we suggest that beginning writers study Gary Provost's *Make Every Word Count* and other basic books (see Bibliography). Consider also enrolling in a writing course taught by an experienced professional who can review your columns and proposal.

Before you enter the world of column writing, spend some time thinking about your favorite columns and why you read them. What about the subject matter draws you in? The writing? The format? Is there a columnist whose style inspires you to sit down at the typewriter? Perhaps later on you'll want to incorporate into your own column some of the elements that appeal to you. Start analyzing and clipping your favorite columns. We'll ask you to take a closer look at them later.

Now turn to Chapter One.

1

The Lure of Column Writing

Columns are short, to-the-point pieces, consistently packaged in a set format and layout, and almost always penned by the same writer or collaborative team. Columns, unlike news and feature stories, regularly reside in the same spot in a publication and can contain opinion. While newspapers purchase by far the greatest number of columns, magazines and, to a lesser extent, newsletters also carry them. Some newspaper columns are staff-written; others are contributed by local writers. Still others are brokered by syndicates or by the writer, who sells the column to many publications at a time.

Column length depends on the subject matter, the kind of publication, and, for some newspaper columns, the amount of space available in that day's issue. Newspaper social and political commentary tends to run about 750 to 1,000 words, while other columns may be as short as 500 words or as long as

1,200. Magazines often allow lengthier columns, while newsletters, with their limited space, generally opt for smaller ones.

Naturally, the frequency of the publication puts an upper limit on the number of times a column appears. Other than that, how often a column reaches print is based on whatever agreement writer and editor reach.

> *"If I started writing a history of the world, it would taper off at 700 words and end at 750."*—*Fred Reed,* Washington Times *science and soldiering columnist.*

> *Syndicated food columnist Jane Stern's advice for beginning food writers: "Buy clothing with elastic waistbands."*

> *On writing a personalities column: "It's no gateway to popularity among the rich and famous."*—*Bill Speers, columnist for the Philadelphia* Inquirer.

A column can be advice to the lovelorn, hints for keeping your canary healthy, information on buying computers and software, a political discourse on world affairs, commentary on last night's baseball game, instructions for playing a bridge hand, a personal reminiscence on growing up in rural Vermont, decorating ideas, beauty tips, fashion news.

A column can take any of several formats: narrative (such as Art Buchwald's, George Will's, and Jack Anderson's columns), question-and-answer (Ann Landers's), bits-and-pieces (Lloyd Shearer's "Intelligence Report" in *Parade*), how-to's (Barbara Gibbons's "Slim Gourmet"), catalogues (Elizabeth Gaynor's "Buys of the Week" in *Parade*), and games (Charles Goren's "On Bridge"). The format a writer selects depends on the column's purpose, the way the writer chooses to convey the information, the writer's style, and the editor's needs.

The Rewards of Column Writing

Many writers aspire to become columnists. And it's easy to see why. When you're as widely read and controversial as Mike Royko, for example, you might, as he has, earn a mention in the comic strip *Shoe*. A William F. Buckley can command a five-figure fee for less than an hour's worth of public speaking. Think of how many times a day Ann Landers and Abigail Van Buren are quoted over back fences, by water coolers, and in bowling alleys. And how much easier it is for a Russell Baker than for the average freelancer to land a book contract.

While the dream of superstar status propels our pens, column writing offers many rewards besides celebrity and riches. The best part for most columnists is having a forum in which to air opinions, to shape people's thoughts, and to change their lives. The local commentator who takes a stand against building a highway through an established neighborhood may influence a crucial vote or spur a citizens' committee into motion. An action-line columnist can keep shady businesses from taking advantage of unsuspecting consumers.

Single-parenting columnist and author Stephen Atlas uses his weekly column on raising children on one's own to dispense his philosophy that single parenting can be a positive experience. "I feel that my column can make a difference in people's lives," says Atlas. "I have a forum where I can show people that they are not alone, that they can improve their lives."

Along with the mantel of columnist comes freedom—the freedom to choose your topics and to voice your opinions. What you put in your column is limited only by your feature's overall subject matter and length, libel laws, good taste, and whatever agreement you've reached with your editor. For example, *The* (Baltimore) *Evening Sun* photography columnist Bonnie J. Schupp can write on any facet of her craft as long as the subject matter is not x-rated.

Syndicated columnist Richard Cohen on what makes a good commentary writer: "Columnists come and go. The guys who stay are the ones who write fast and know how to deal with a variety of subjects."

Commentators have an even freer hand, covering everything from politics and social concerns to personal experiences. That's why William Safire can lash out on one day at the recording industry and its glorification of drugs and kinky sex and on the next write about the intrigues of a Russian grand master chess match, comparing the USSR game tactics to Soviet politics.

Other than general commentators, most columnists stay within one subject area. Since they have to stay on top of their field, they must constantly research their subjects and come up with fresh topics or new approaches to old ones. If you love your subject, it's a wonderful opportunity—like a chocoholic's being told by the doctor to eat more of the confection. A columnist's expertise grows with every column inch he or she writes. "Writing a column keeps me current," says financial columnist Bob Russell. "I know what's happening in my field, what's happening on the cutting edge."

Fixed deadlines and steady remuneration are additional benefits. Having a regular column, as opposed to relying solely on the hit-or-miss of freelancing articles, provides a stable base around which you can organize writing time. Instead of hanging around the mailbox, waiting for the next assignment, you've got work to do. Each New Year's Day, restaurateur and Chicago *Sun Times*'s food columnist Chef Louis Szathmary looks in his mirror as he shaves and delights in telling himself, "You have fifty-two columns to write. You have something to do this year." And even if the payment for the column isn't going to put you on the French Riviera, it will provide at least some dependable income while you're pursuing a career in the erratic field of freelance writing.

Freelancers also find assignments roll in more readily when their credentials include the word *columnist*. A regular column demonstrates a certain professionalism and track record. In other words, if you've been trusted to deliver an ongoing feature by one editor, another one will feel that awarding you a one-shot assignment is less of a gamble.

High visibility is another reward of column writing. Few readers recall the names of news and feature reporters, but they do remember columnists, and look to them as experts. Also, columnists whose photos appear next to their bylines often become local celebrities, with people stopping them on the street and in the supermarket.

Thus, columnists develop followings. *Working Woman* columnist and author Betty Lehan Harragan, whose column offers expert opinion on negotiating the ins and outs of the business world, has devoted readers all over the country who rush to hear her lectures. Georgia anglers stow away Charles Salter's Atlanta *Constitution* fishing column in billfolds and dresser drawers, waiting for the right season to test that new lure or line.

As a newspaper columnist's reputation builds, so does the possibility of national syndication—having a column appear in several or many newspapers on an ongoing basis. For example, for years *Washington Post* readers eagerly sought out Richard Cohen's commentary on the two mornings a week it appeared on the front page of the Metro section. So broad was Cohen's appeal that the Washington Post Writers Group syndicate enlisted him. Now Cohen reaches readers from coast to coast. And as a result, his income has increased and his name is on even more lips.

Career Opportunities

Column writing jobs are the cream of the journalism world, the position many rank-and-file writers aspire to. And, indeed, many columnists do come up this way, starting as newspaper staff reporters. Sometimes they take on columnist duties gradually, continuing to report the news until they work their way up to full-time columnist. Richard Cohen and social commentator Roger Simon both began their careers covering the news before going on to staff columnist positions and then national syndication.

Freelancers, on the other hand, generally become columnists in one of two ways. Either they have expertise in some field and are asked to do a column on it or they come up with a good idea and a solid proposal for a column that entices an editor.

In the late 1970s Stephen Atlas's marriage crumbled, and his young son and daughter went to live with their mother hundreds of miles away. To ease his loneliness, Atlas set up a singles group for art lovers and became an active member of Parents Without Partners. A few years later Atlas used his experience to pen a resource guide for single parents. Flushed with success, he then developed a proposal for an advice column for single parents and sent it off to *The* (Baltimore) *Sun*. The column made its debut in March 1981 and at its peak appeared in more than seventy newspapers across the country.

On the other hand, Rita St. Clair was running a successful interior design business and had just been elected president of the American Society of Interior Designers. As chief officer, she traveled extensively, speaking and giving interviews from coast to coast. Enter the Los Angeles Times Syndicate, looking for someone to take over its "Designing Woman" column. In its search, the syndicate contacted editors around the country, requesting nominations. "Ask Rita St. Clair," they chorused, "she has opinions." Today readers in more than 150 papers throughout the United States and the United Kingdom see her byline each week.

Columnists' earnings vary tremendously, depending primarily on the publication's circulation and frequency. The bigger-circulation publications usually pay better for columns, just as they do for freelance articles. A small-town newspaper may offer no more than $5 per installment, while a larger one might pay $25 and up. The size of the check also depends on how often the column appears and its length. The columnist's popularity, expertise, and, in the case of lesser-known freelancers, writing credentials also play a role in establishing fees.

Columnists working full-time for a publication can earn anywhere from $10,000 a year on small weeklies to $50,000 and more on large papers. The earnings of syndicated and self-syndicated columnists vary according to the number of markets the column is sold to. A feature can command as much as $75 per installment or as little as $2 from each one, again based on the size of the newspaper or magazine, the publication's circulation, the writer's popularity, and, in the case of self-syndicators, the writer's skill as a negotiator. Those very few at the pinnacle of the syndicated world can earn $150,000 or more per year.

If becoming a superstar, a Buchwald or Bombeck, is your goal, aim for the top, but keep in mind that few writers scale the dazzling heights. For many columnists the riches are modest, a supplemental income rather than a living wage. As for fame, many syndicated and magazine columnists end up leaders in their field but not household names, while small-town columnists find a certain celebrity status among friends, neighbors, and the local public. For them, the glory comes from succeeding at making it into print, doing a top-notch column, and having it well received.

What Does It Take to Be a Columnist?

The ability to work quickly and write concisely. To write a column, you must know that you can write regularly, consistently, and quickly enough to meet your obligations. Count on constant deadlines and a scramble to come up with ideas, research them, and get them onto paper. Successful columnists warm to this challenge.

> *"In science, people like seeing held views challenged."*— *Fred Reed,* Washington Times *science and soldiering columnist.*

A style. A strong style—smooth, colorful prose injected with the writer's personality—separates the master columnists from the hacks. Tricks of the trade, such as varying sentence lengths, using concrete images and words, and conversing directly with the reader, bring even the most pedestrian subjects to life. Can you imagine a food piece by Calvin Trillin without his customary lip smacking? And it's Heloise's neighborly common sense with its push-up-your-shirtsleeves-and-let's-get-it-done attitude that keeps homeowners looking to her for advice. A unique style seldom happens overnight but rather is developed over a period of time through practice and conscious self-evaluation.

An opinion or point of view. "There's a bullheadedness," says *Washington Times* science and soldiering columnist Fred Reed. "I think it takes a certain amount of 'This, by God, is how the world is.' " A columnist must have an opinion or a point of view, state it, and be willing to take the flak that may come from giving it. Wishy-washy won't do. While a few kinds of columns, such as small-town society goings on, "it happened fifty years ago today" listings, and word games don't take positions, most columns, even those on household hints, home repair, beauty, and television, proffer an author's views.

To Consider: Before going on to the next chapter, answer the following questions.

1. Why do I want to write a column?
2. Do I have an idea about what I want to do a column on?
3. Am I good at generating ideas?
4. Do I have enough self-discipline to turn out a column on a regular basis?
5. How badly do I want to do this? What am I willing to give up?
6. Do I have, or can I develop, a network for getting the information I need?
7. Can I deal with the possibility of low pay for my column?
8. Can I meet constant deadlines? Can I cope with the stress?
9. Can I deal with problems of publication, for example: fickle audiences, publication politics, shifts in editors, and changes in the marketplace?

10. How will my writing a column affect my family? Economically? Time spent together? Changing family routine?

After you've given the above questions careful thought and have decided to try out the job of columnist, you'll be joining a club that has many happy members. Now turn to Chapter Two to begin your career.

2

Deciding on the Column You Want to Write

When you picked up this book, maybe you already had an inkling of the subject matter, form, or purpose of a column you wanted to do. Or, perhaps you knew what kind of publication you'd like to write for. As you generate and develop a column idea, consider the advice of syndicated consumer columnist Martin Sloane on how to find a gap in the market. "I'd interview readers of newspapers. 'What isn't in the paper that you'd like to see?' I'd ask them. The bottom line is finding a subject that someone's going to read." Of course, you must also find a subject you're equipped to write about. If you uncover a great need for an auto repair column but don't know mufflers from brake shoes, obviously that idea won't work for you. However, if several people mentioned an education column geared toward parents of school-aged children and you've just sent your fourth child off to kindergarten, that's a possible subject.

Sometimes just looking around your community will lead to a germ of a column idea. In 1976, Sue Rusche's comfortable Atlanta neighborhood was rocked by the revelation that several ten- and eleven-year-old children were experimenting with drugs. Also, head shops had opened nearby, luring kids with pipes, roach clips, bongs, and other drug paraphernalia. Rusche was worried. What could she do to keep her own youngsters and others' from entering that netherworld of illicit drugs? In answer, she founded a drug-addiction prevention program called Families in Action, authored a manual on forming similar groups around the country, and started *Drug Abuse Update*, a quarterly publication consisting of abstracts from medical journals. Finally, her concerns led her to the idea of doing a syndicated column. "I wanted to get out good information that would counteract the 'use drugs' messages that are out there," Rusche says. In 1983 she approached King Features, and today her column appears in more than seventy papers throughout the United States.

A solid idea is crucial if you hope to succeed as a columnist. Even if you already have a general column idea in mind, you'll probably have to refine and focus it. As you develop your idea, consider these points:

Choose a fresh slant or subject. Some fields, such as dieting, nutrition, sports, business, books, and personal advice, will forever draw readers. Although earthquakes may shake China and ocean waters eat away Atlantic coastlines, Anne and Alan Average will still want to know how to prune their boxwood or how to work off an extra ten pounds. However, if you latch onto an evergreen, you'll need to bring a fresh perspective to it, as Dr. Ruth Westheimer did by taking the tried and true subject of personal advice and giving it a new twist, coming up with her sex question-and-answer offering.

Yet even as old standbys continue to attract faithful audiences, trends in life-styles, developments in technology, and problems of modern existence generate new column subjects. For instance, the current popularity of personal computers has opened up a whole new market for columnists who know RAM from ROM. However, the prevalence of computer columns may wane, as did those on CB radios, which were all the rage back in the 1970s. The challenge is to catch a trend just as it begins to take on momentum.

Choose a subject you're interested in. Remember that you'll have to write on this subject daily, weekly, or monthly for a number of years. You'll find the column will follow you wherever you go—you'll muse about it while driving along the interstate; you'll think about it on family outings; you'll ponder it as you brush you teeth. So, by all means, pick a subject you want as a constant companion.

Choose a subject you know about. Interest alone is not enough to carry off most kinds of columns. True, you could sustain a general question-and-answer feature with strong curiosity and good research. But for most subjects—real estate, medicine, business, home repair, and so on—you'll need a solid foundation in the field to speak with authority. You'll also have to keep on top of the newest trends, products, and information. Readers depend on writers' expertise to make purchases, form opinions, solve problems, and learn new skills, and they have every right to expect accurate information.

> *"Outdoor writers are expected to be able to get out and do these things [the sports they write about]. If you can't, people who do know them can kind of sniff you out . . . I don't know whether I'm a fisherman that likes to write or a writer that likes to fish."—Joe Doggett, outdoors columnist for the Houston* Chronicle.

"The first responsibility of a columnist is to speak with authority on your subject," says business columnist Betty Lehan Harragan. "If the column is on finance, then you should be writing it because you've worked in finance and are deeply involved." Without being an expert on your subject, she asks, how can you know which of the information you get from research and interviews is accurate?

Simply growing a philodendron in your living room doesn't mean you can advise readers on general plant care. On the other hand, a *serious* hobby can be parlayed into a column.

Suppose you work as a supervisor for a bridge construction firm but at day's end can't wait to rush home to the greenhouse you've built in your backyard. Over the years you've developed a small business selling plants to people in your area. The town paper once even ran a feature on you, complete with photographs. Your know-how could provide enough material for a local column that would interest the apartment dweller whose spider plants are turning brown, the retiree who hopes to coax blooms from a cactus, or the restaurant owner who wants to dress up the entrance with potted ferns.

Keep in mind, too, that you might be able to ghostwrite a column for an established expert or collaborate with another writer knowledgeable on a certain subject. We'll explain how ghosting and collaboration work more fully later in this chapter.

Consider how much and what kind of research you want to do. Subjects such as community happenings or personalities require legwork and interviews. Other subjects demand even deeper digging. Syndicated consumer columnist Martin Sloane has the telephone to his ear constantly, going to bat for consumers. Even commentators such as Richard Cohen and Roger Simon keep phone lines humming as they track down stories, check rumors, and verify statements.

Although personal philosophy pieces and some humor columns can come straight from your own experiences and thoughts, for most columns, no matter how much expertise you have, you'll need to spend time searching out facts and poring over new studies. So when planning for your column, remember to allow time in your schedule for research. Err on the conservative side, estimating a larger chunk than you think you'll need. You'll find people rattle on longer than you expect, busy signals delay you, reference books are elusive, and research defies interpretation.

When business and games columnist Bob Russell decided to write a "person in the street" column for the *Columbia Flier*, a Maryland weekly, he figured it would be a snap. He would come up with a question for each issue, ask a few people their opinions, and write up the answers. How long could it take? He soon found out. Armed with a query about local politics, he set out for the shopping mall to get quick replies from a few shoppers. Instead, he found that some didn't understand the question, others came from out of town and knew nothing about the subject, and still others wanted to hash over the fine points of the issue in agonizing detail. He then transferred his attack to the downtown lakefront, where again he had more misses than hits. What should have been a breeze rapidly became an albatross. Wisely, Russell canned the column and used the time for other, more lucrative, writing pursuits.

Focusing Your Idea

The more carefully focused your idea, the greater your chances of success as a columnist. Try these strategies to help you refine your column idea.

Restrict your subject. Once you've chosen a general field, try to narrow it down. In an area like business, for example, consider concentrating on a specialty such as personal finance, stocks and bonds, company news. Food writers, for instance, can limit their scope to health foods, diet foods, microwave cooking, regional recipes, or presentation of meals.

Even humorists can choose to confine their columns. Erma Bombeck uses the milieu of the housewife as a frame for her observations, and Art Buchwald tends to hook his column to federal politics and timely issues. (On the other hand, general humor writer Dave Barry lets his mind and pen roam throughout the universe, writing on subjects ranging from Cleveland's proposed Rock 'n' Roll Hall of Fame to the Nautilus craze to the IRS.)

If you need help generating angles, look in a variety of newspapers, magazines, and newsletters for columns and articles on your subject. Suppose you want to write a travel column. Go through newspapers (not just the ones you read regularly but out-of-town papers as well), travel monthlies such as *Travel-Holiday* and *Travel & Leisure*, in-flight magazines, and food and drink periodicals. Don't forget general publications such as *The Saturday Evening Post* and women's magazines. As you read each article, look at the slant and decide if it's a possible angle for your column subject. Or does it suggest one? A feature about traveling with pets might make you, the owner of six dogs, four cats, and seventeen rabbits, realize that the author has just skimmed the surface of the subject and that you could easily come up with 800 words a month for the next five years on animal carriers, nutrition on the road, locating a vet in a strange city, finding accommodations that will accept both you and Fido, preparing Kitty for a plane ride to St. Croix, choosing a rabbit-sitter who will love Fluffy, Hoppy, and Jumpy as much as you do.

To Do: Write your general column subject at the head of a page of blank paper. Now come up with as many different slants for your subject as you can. Don't censor ideas; just list them.

Tailor your subject to a particular readership. A creative choice of audience can give a column its slant. A science writer could gear a column to school children, housewives, business people, scientists, or to the general public. A business writer could aim for retirees, investors, or a broad readership. Jerry Feigen, using his expertise in venture capital, directs his financial column in *In Business* toward the entrepreneurs who read the magazine. Conversely, *Washington Times* soldiering columnist Fred Reed took what would normally be a technical subject written for military personnel in a specialized publication and pointed it at the readers of a daily newspaper.

To Do: Headline another clean sheet of paper with your general subject. Now list ten to twenty possible audiences. Keep an open mind, and don't limit your picks to the obvious. The first five or so groups should come easily, but then you'll probably have to push yourself. Could your potential audiences include children? teenagers? women? men? young adults? senior citizens? a particular ethnic group? parents? step-parents? animal owners? boaters? Iowans? doctors? lawyers? Indian chiefs?
Now let's see if you can come up with an angle for each. For

instance, take an outdoor recreation feature. You could certainly imagine a general approach for most of the audiences, such as "what's new in recreation for women," "what's new in recreation for seniors," "what's new in recreation for doctors." Now push your mind a little farther. What about an outdoor family activity column geared toward parents with preschoolers? A recreation column for the physically handicapped? A consumer column evaluating sports equipment and discussing new products for wealthy people? A snowmobile column for Minnesotans?

Keep this list, along with your first one, on your desk (if it's not too cluttered), the kitchen table, a bulletin board, or even taped to a mirror—anywhere in view. Keeping the lists visible helps jog your brain and lets you add to them whenever another slant or potential audience occurs to you. Plan to spend some time seriously pondering the possibilities, If joining the ranks of columnists is an immediate goal, then set a deadline for deciding which slant appeals most. If embarking on your new career is farther down the road, then you'll have more leisure to contemplate your choice—although remember, what is "in" today may be passé tomorrow.

Decide on a purpose. While your mind is percolating with slants and audiences, start thinking about the purpose of your column. Do you want to provide information, as in a general question-and-answer or personalities column? Do you want to entertain à la Burton Hillis in *Good Housekeeping* or Joey Adams in the *New York Post*? Do you want to rouse people to action? Do you want to give advice—about pet care, health, or careers? Your mission as a columnist will help you select slant and subject. (Shortly, we'll discuss how your purpose will also affect your selection of format.)

Pick a title. A good overall title can act as a focusing mechanism, setting a tone or mood and encapsulating the subject. A title like "Dear Abby," the salutation with which readers start their letters to Abigail Van Buren, clues us in that this will be a feature filled with personal letters from readers and that the tone will be informal. "Dear Ms. Van Buren" would put distance between the columnist and her correspondents. Joe Graedon's "People's Pharmacy" suggests a concerned neigh-

borhood pharmacist surrounded by consumers waiting to ask
questions. "Fight Back" is a perfect name for Dave Horowitz's
syndicated consumer advocacy column, which points up
problems, alerts consumers to dangerous products, and offers
helpful information for wise consumerism. Susan Dietz's syndicated "Single File" column for unmarrieds makes good use
of a pun and a picture. Stan Jones's computer column in Fairbanks, Alaska's *News-Miner* sports "Random Access" as its title.

*Joseph Spear, syndicated investigative columnist and
editor for the Jack Anderson organization on becoming
an investigative writer: "You have to have a desire to do
public service. You must believe in the free press and the
people's right to know—in your heart, not just as an aca-
demic exercise."*

Most of us have to think long and hard to come up with an
appropriate appellation. But, for a lucky few, a title was just
hanging there, waiting to be plucked. Associated Press sports-
writer Hal Bock pens a column named "Bock's Score." Sports-
writer Richard Gutwillig of the Gannett Westchester-
Rockland chain, whose friends for years have called him "Gut,"
writes, what else? "Gut Reactions." Susan Subtle of the San
Francisco *Chronicle* puts together a consumer catalogue feature with photos of good buys named "The Subtle Shopper."
And A. J. Hand pens a do-it-yourself column called, of course,
"Hand Around the House."

Try to come up with a catchy moniker for your feature. Test
metaphors, clever twists on words, a takeoff on your name, a
concise phrase describing the column. Think of the title as a
working one, since it may never make it into print. Many
published columns carry only the columnist's name or a title
chosen by an editor. However, a snappy handle may catch an
editor's eye when you market your feature and may go on to
headline your column in the paper.

Make sure your topic is one you can sustain. Once you've
selected your subject and slant, or at least narrowed your
choices to two or three, ask yourself whether each one is a tru-

ly valid column idea. Could you sustain it, coming up with enough information and subtopics to keep rolling for years? "Dear Abby" can go on forever, because the topic is never ending—people and their problems. Then, too, the constant flow of letters keeps the idea bank replenished. On the other hand, a column on the history of state flags, profiling a different one each week, wouldn't work because there's only enough fodder for a year. However, changing the approach to highlighting a historical happening from a particular state each week would allow you to go on forever.

How long an idea will last is also related to how frequently the column is going to appear. Does the topic lend itself to a daily, weekly, or monthly airing? As a rule, the more general the column subject, the more subtopics you can generate and the more installments you can write. On the other hand, a column on arthritis probably wouldn't work as a daily feature because after you've covered the basics—the different forms, whom it affects, treatments, and research to date—you'd be left scrambling for material. So it might be more realistic to write on this subject for a weekly.

Choosing a Format

Another way to focus a subject is to decide what kind of format you want to use. Your choice will depend on what best suits your subject, purpose, audience, and, equally important, your personality and writing style. Below, we've listed the most common ways of setting up a column. Note that some categories overlap.

NARRATIVES A straight essay, generally containing philosophical musings or commentary, either serious or humorous. This form is one of the most difficult kinds of columns to write. A writer of narrative must have a sharp, analytical mind capable of developing an idea and carrying it through smoothly, without detour, to its conclusion in a limited number of words. An individual style combined with a personal view of the world provides the foundation and framework for this kind of commentary.

Opinion narrative—An essay form in which the writer expresses an opinion, whether the topic is politics, social issues, religion, business, sports, television, music, art, etc. In this form, the columnist clearly states the issue in the first few paragraphs, then articulates a particular point of view, supporting the argument with facts, statistics, and/or anecdotes. Examples of narrative opinion columnists are Evans and Novak, William F. Buckley, Mary McGrory, Richard Cohen, George Will, Roger Simon, William Safire, Ellen Goodman, Vicki Williams, and sports commentator Dick Young.

Personal essay narrative—A discourse in which the writer recounts a personal experience or reflects upon something that has affected him or her. Warning: This form looks deceptively easy. To tackle this format you must draw readers in through your writing personality and hold their interest even if the subject by itself might not ordinarily grab a reader. Over the years, *House Beautiful* columnist Dee Hardie has formed a bond with her readers through her expressive and highly reflective style. So she is able to write about hot water bottles, Harvey the gardener, aprons, and baskets and still have her fans clamoring for more. Other writers who use this format are Andy Rooney, Lois Wyse, Erma Bombeck. Roger Rosenblatt's "Revenge My Sweet," reprinted in Chapter Three, is a good example of this form.

Informational narrative—A narrative packed with facts and advice to inform readers or help them make decisions. Emphasis here is on service—presenting useful, solid information in a logical, readable manner. Whether an installment begins with an anecdote, a direct statement, or a statistic, the reader should know within a few lines what the piece will cover. Obviously, you must have a strong background in your field to write an informational column telling readers about the ins and outs of planning a nutritious diet, hiring office personnel, choosing a vacation spot, purchasing a condominium, or whatever. Examples of this type of format are Sylvia Porter's money column, Dr. Jean Mayer and Jeanne Goldberg's nutrition pieces, Stephen Birnbaum's travel features, and Lew Sichelman's real estate writings.

Profile narrative—A portrait of a person, usually a celebrity, painted in words. Here the writer must capture the essence of an individual, using keen observation to pick up the person's habits, quirks, mannerisms, sound of voice, speech patterns, physical appearance, and surroundings. A quick ear and fast pen should latch onto the subject's more self-revealing quotes to fill out the portrait, and all of this must be skillfully conveyed to the reader. James Brady's personality pieces in *Parade* are narrative profiles.

Extended-anecdote narrative—A column made up of a single incident that tells a story. Columnists who use this format must have a fiction writer's skill in characterization, pacing, dialogue, and description. Veterans like Calvin Trillin, Erma Bombeck, and Roger Simon use this device to entertain or to make a point or statement about life. This method enables commentators, in particular, to get a message across without a lot of noise. The writer simply tells the story and maybe adds a few comments, allowing readers to draw their own conclusions. For example, in one column, a poignant tale of a hungry man arrested for shoplifting a package of sweet rolls, Roger Simon leads readers into the store to watch the starving man wolf down the pastry. Bringing the readers along as witnesses, he follows the "miscreant" down the byways of justice to the jailhouse and then to the courtroom, where the man is sentenced to three days in the slammer. In the end, Simon has his audience as irritated with society's lack of concern for the poor as he is. Had Simon just talked about the event, without pulling his readers into the scene, the tone would have probably come across as preachy and the column wouldn't have been so effective.

Conversational narrative—A format consisting of imaginary conversations among characters. The discussion, which centers around a particular subject or situation, serves to express the author's viewpoint. Satirist Art Buchwald reigns supreme over this tricky format. For example, one day Buchwald will invite us into his home to listen to "him and his wife" talk disdainfully about America's obsession with English royalty, all the while keeping an eye peeled for the mail carrier who, maybe, just maybe, will bring them a coveted invitation to party with Princess Di and Prince Charles. Another day he'll have readers eavesdrop on a conversation between worried citizen Selwyn Barnaby (who fears that use of the military for drug surveillance will lead to tanks on Main Street and a spy at every window) and a gung-ho patriot who is ever ready to justify Uncle Sam's behavior, no matter how bold or bizarre, in the war against the weed. Not only is Buchwald a master of dialogue but he also sets a scene and puts action behind his conversations. In his columns, people don't just sit around and yak; they get caught up in events swirling around them. Another writer who employs this technique is Lawrence Block, who engages in verbal exchanges with his classroom of fictional students, featuring the ever-inquisitive Arnold, Mimi, and Rachel. He uses the device as a springboard for discussions of fiction writing techniques in his monthly *Writer's Digest* column.

While conversation appears to be an easy way to get a point across, in less-skilled hands than Buchwald's and Block's, it becomes sophomoric and tedious. Don't look to this format as a way to make writing your column easier; if anything, it presents a greater challenge. Instead of communicating in flowing prose where you have room to manipulate words and thoughts, you must rely on the clipped phrases of conversation. Every sentence must have a purpose, and all the information must be packaged in dialogue. Like a good novelist, this kind of columnist must know how to duplicate the natural rhythms of speech, sensing what to keep in and what to cut out.

QUESTION-AND-ANSWER A column where the writer answers readers' mailed-in questions. This type of column can consist of one question with a detailed answer or several queries with shorter replies. Q&A columns depend on reader participation. When the letters come in, the author must choose which to print, then research and capsulize the answers. There are several versions of the Q&A:

Advice Q&A—A form in which the columnist offers counsel for readers' problems. The superstars of the question-and-answer world are personal advice columnists Ann Landers and Abigail Van Buren (Dear Abby), but writers in many other fields such as health, pet care, careers, finance, consumer issues, decorating, and antiques, use this format, too. Billy Graham's daily one-question syndicated column provides counseling with a Christian viewpoint for people with personal problems and religious concerns. Elizabeth L. Post follows her grandmother-in-law's penstrokes, answering readers' queries about matters of etiquette, while Judith Martin's Miss Manners offers an interesting twist, with tongue-in-cheek pointers on proper social conduct.

Action-line Q&A—A variation of the question-and-answer advice format. Here readers write in and complain about roofs that leak, coffee pots that don't perk, potholes that need patching, and money not refunded for goods returned. Unlike standard Q&A columnists, action-line writers dash to the rescue of mistreated, frustrated, and bewildered consumers, delving into the situation, solving problems, and dispensing helpful information. Newspapers all over the country carry this type of column as a service to their readership.

An exotic hybrid is Percy Ross's column "Thanks a Million." Troubled readers write in describing their plights, but instead of just handing out advice like Ann Landers or acting solely like an action line advocate, Ross donates money to letter writers whose causes he determines are worthy of his philanthropy. It helps to be a millionaire or have some private source of money to pull off this kind of off-beat feature.

Informational Q&A—A column that provides information with no advice. An insatiable curiosity and good researching skills, along with a talent for capsulizing replies, marks the successful columnist in this format. "Ask Andy" creator Ed Grade answers queries from young readers on such diverse subjects as how is a diamond formed? when did the first Chamber of Commerce open? and how many Supreme Court justices have sat on the bench? He boils down replies to these and other mysteries to a few concise sentences. Another version of the

Q&A informational column is Walter Scott's "Personality Parade," which has been quenching *Parade* readers' thirst for knowledge about the rich and famous by unearthing facts and presenting them in a few straightforward lines.

Profile Q&A—A close-up look at one person, often a celebrity, where the writer presents in print both the writer's questions and the subject's answers. The simplest way of doing this type of column is a version of fill-in-the blanks. The writer develops a fixed set of questions and repeats them to each new subject interviewed, always asking more questions than needed so that even if some answers are duds, there is still a selection to draw from to fill the column space. This type of treatment is not meant to portray a personality in depth but rather to present a surface look. Syndicated columnist Cheryl Lavin writes this kind of feature, turning her spotlight on Hollywood entertainers.

A Q&A profile can also be a shorter version of its bigger sibling, the question-and-answer interview found in magazines like *Playboy*. A few pointed questions, tailored to the subject and followed by his or her revealing answers, present readers with a fuller descriptive picture of the interviewee. Again, the writer poses more questions than will be printed and often edits the replies, cutting out repetitions, correcting grammar, and clarifying meanings.

BITS-AND-PIECES A column made up of short items, sometimes related, sometimes not. Society and personality features frequently take this form, but subjects ranging from politics to sports can be tailored to this framework, as well. John Naisbitt uses this setup in a syndicated column highlighting business trends. Nostalgia features, where readers learn what happened ten, twenty, fifty years ago today, also fit this mold.

The length of items within each bits-and-pieces installment can fluctuate or be fairly consistent, depending on the author's style and the subject matter. In his *Parade* magazine "Intelligence Report" column, Lloyd Shearer varies the length of his potpourri of items from 50 words to 500, based on the complexity of the subject.

READER DIALOGUE A column in which readers send in stories
of funny things that have happened to them, tales of woe, opinions on current issues, tidbits of information, helpful hints, reports on community happenings. This format differs from bits-
and-pieces in that the voices of readers who contribute to the
column come through along with that of the columnist. The
column can concentrate on one subject or not. Heloise, for example, focuses on household hints, answering questions,
printing readers' suggestions, and commenting on them. "Bob
Levey's Washington" in *The Washington Post*, on the other
hand, encompasses many different subjects of interest to the
District of Columbia community. He and his readers argue,
muse over life's vagaries, report on the latest tussle with the
bus system, sing praises of good samaritans helping stranded
motorists, exhort Washingtonians to make donations to Children's Hospital. His column is chock-full of anecdotes, puns,
humorous tidbits, offbeat incidents, and miscellaneous facts.

HOW-TO An instructional piece, usually written in recipe style,
with step-by-step directions. It can be set up with a reader's question serving as an introduction to a long explanation,
as a series of questions with short how-to answers, as a straight
narrative with introductory comments, or as a collection of
tips. In showing how to do something, the writer lists materials needed, tells where to obtain them (when necessary), and
details clear, logical directions. The writer notes potential
problems, suggests what the finished results of the project will
be, and provides helpful illustrations where required. Chicago
Sun-Times columnist Chef Louis Szathmary uses this format,
prefacing his recipes with a several-paragraph lead delineating
the heritage of a dish, offering a few words about its creator,
discussing the cuisine of a region, or discoursing on whatever
he feels will enhance the recipe to follow.

CATALOGUE A quasi-column with a strong visual format, usually
consisting of photographs or illustrations with extended cap-
tions. In this format a picture is worth a lot of words, but
doesn't replace them totally. Getting pertinent information
across in a sentence or two calls for economy of prose. Clever-

ness and wit often add flair to what could be cut-and-dried writing. Fashion, beauty, and consumer columns frequently employ this layout to highlight new products. *New York Magazine*'s "Best Buys" by Corky Pollan and *Family Circle*'s "Finds" are examples of this genre.

GAMES A catchall category for quizzes, puzzles, activities, and game-playing strategies. Illustrations are often a necessary part of the package. Penning bridge columns like Charles Goren's and Alfred Sheinwold's requires an expert knowledge of the game and the talent to express concepts clearly and concisely. Putting together trivia and other kinds of quizzes takes research skills and the ability to phrase questions, keeping them short but including all necessary information. The setup you choose will depend on the game—anagram, cryptogram, riddle, map puzzle, fill-in-the-blank, whatever. This type of feature is limited only by your imagination and by what's already being done.

To Do: Before you do this exercise, you must have decided on an overall column subject. Look back at your lists on slant and audience. One of the ideas should be jumping out, waving its arms at you. If none is, pick one anyhow for the purpose of this exercise. Maybe running through this drill will help you make up your mind.

Now read through the above format possibilities again. Imagine your column in each of these different setups. Which would work? Which wouldn't, and why? Again, don't be limited by the obvious. Play around with your subject and the various setups. Keep in mind that sometimes formats can be combined. For example, a home repair column can open with a discourse on fall cleaning of gutters and then proceed with readers' questions on other aspects of do-it-yourself projects. A bits-and-pieces design can be combined with reader participation for a lively nostalgia column.

Jot down a list of potential formats for your feature and pin it up next to your slant and audience lists. Add to it over the next week or so.

Putting It All Together

Now it's time to clothe your subject and slant in several different formats to find the one that looks best.

To Do: Write or type your column subject across the top of a sheet
of paper. Beneath it list as many topics for individual columns as
you can think of, a minimum of twenty ideas. For example, if
your column is general beauty tips, you might list:
    new products for your hair
    eyelash dying
    long-lasting nail polish
    pedicures
    choosing moisturizers
    minimizing the effects of the sun on your skin
    henna rinses
    joining a health club
    antiwrinkle exercises
    choosing a perfume
    cream vs. powder makeups
    makeup and contact lenses
    cosmetic tooth bonding
    permanents
    ear piercing
    shaping eyebrows
If you can't come up with at least twenty ideas right away, maybe you need to rethink your subject.

Now choose one of the ideas to write about, and circle it. Try
to pick one that excites you and that's typical of the kind of column you envision. In other words, leave the oddball topic out for
now. Take some time to think about the idea and what you
want to say about it.

Next look back over your list of formats. Which seem best or
most natural for the kind of column you want to do? Pick two or
more to try.

Now take out some clean sheets of paper, headlining each

one with the idea you've circled. Try sketching out the idea in the formats you've chosen. For example, a beauty column on vitamins and your skin could be written as one complete narrative or as a general discussion. Or it could be presented in a bits-and-pieces format with one section on Vitamin A, one on Vitamin E, and so on. Or a bits-and-pieces could be divided into sections discussing short topics like how vitamins improve skin tone, prevent skin disease, eliminate dryness.

Map out a rough draft in each format. Don't worry about spelling, grammar, punctuation, smooth prose, or getting facts right. This is merely a test drive, a way of trying out a few setups. No one's going to read this but you.

Once you've done these, review your list of formats and select one or two of the least likely candidates and repeat the process. Don't worry if a marriage of your subject and a particular format seems absurd; give it a go. What you're attempting to come up with is a unique combination, and to do this you've got to break out of established patterns of thinking.

One of the most creative ideas to come across our desks was George R. Plagenz's column "A Stranger Goes to Church" that appeared in the *Columbus* (Ohio) *Citizen-Journal*. In this feature the author graded churches the way restaurant critics do eateries. He attended services and evaluated each religious institution for warmth of its congregation, ambience, and appeal of its service. He wrote up his critique in a narrative and then took it one step farther. Just as AAA rates hotels with diamonds and Michelin grades restaurants with cutlery symbols, Plagenz awarded stars for quality of worship service, sermon, music, and friendliness—three stars for tops, two for pretty good, and so on down the line.

Plagenz didn't come up with this idea by playing it safe. He took a chance and hit gold. What about the formats you've come up with? Are they totally out of the question or did you strike it rich and come up with an original idea? If none of the formats has panned out, dig some more. Keep doing this exercise until you discover the one that fits. You may find, after all your experimenting, that you still want to go with a traditional setup. Or perhaps you'll want to use one format one day, another the next. This is fine as long as you retain continuity and don't confuse your readers.

Two More Options: Ghosting and Collaborating

For some freelance writers the way to get a column is by ghostwriting one for someone else—an expert, public figure, business professional, academician, or celebrity who doesn't have the time and/or the writing talent to draft a regular column. In ghostwriting, you write for another person as if you are that person, translating his or her ideas, tone, and words into a readable column. Collaboration, on the other hand, means dividing writing, researching, and editing tasks with one or more other writers, an expert, a celebrity, or a public figure. Unlike ghosting, where one personality is entirely submerged, collaborating allows both voices to mix and be heard and both names to share the spotlight. Many columns are written by ghosts or collaborative teams, so keep these possibilities in mind.

GHOSTING If you ghostwrite a column, the public doesn't know your name. Your existence, in fact, may be a carefully guarded secret. The other person gets the byline and the glory. What you get is part of the pay. Experienced writers often use ghosting to enhance their career credentials. Novices, on the other hand, find ghosting a way of breaking into print.

Division of labor between "author" and ghost can take a number of forms. Ultimately it depends on what the two of you agree on and contract to do. In some arrangements, the ghost does all the research and writing, presenting it for the "author's" review just before mailing it. In other partnerships, the ghost interviews the "author," honing the words and thoughts into smooth prose. Or sometimes the author does the bulk of the research, giving the writer the material—tapes, drafts, notes—to shape into readable form. With more skilled authors, a ghostwriter may be called on only to edit.

For five years Ruth Glick ghosted a sexual advice column. Glick, an experienced newspaper reporter and freelancer, approached a sex therapist she had profiled in a national magazine and suggested they team up to do a column for that same publication. With the therapist's help, Glick developed a proposal, wrote up several sample columns, and mailed them. The editor agreed to the column and offered Glick and her "author" each a contract. Once the column was established, every month Glick would sort through reader questions with the therapist, get her opinion, write up the column, and send it. For her work, Glick was paid half the fee.

The disadvantage of this type of arrangement, Glick points out, is that "you are at the mercy of the expert. If he decides he doesn't want to do the column anymore, you don't do it anymore." Therefore, she strongly recommends having a written contract between ghost and "author," spelling out duties, pay, and term.

A contract will also ensure that you don't get stuck doing more than your share for the fee. And if you do get dumped on, a written agreement will give you more leverage in negotiating a pay raise. Make sure your personal lawyer looks over the document to see that you get a fair shake. In addition, be sure to try out some sample columns with your "author" before signing on to be a ghost.

The money you receive will be a percentage of the full paycheck issued for the column, a daily or hourly rate, or a per-column allotment. Fees and percentages vary. Established writers with an idea of the time a project will consume and how much they normally earn per hour, set their fees accordingly. Beginners can check *Writer's Market* or call a writers' organization to find out the going rate.

If you're a writer with a column idea but lack expertise on a subject you want to write about, look for an expert wherever authorities in the field gather—associations, universities, agencies, companies, etc.

If you have a column idea but are not a writer and are looking for a ghost, call writers' organizations in your community for referrals. Or phone a local writer whose work you admire and ask if he or she would be willing to do the job. If the writer can't, ask for a referral.

Collaborating. Collaborators are the Everly Brothers of the written word, blending their voices in a column to produce clear, vibrant harmonies. Column partners can parcel out the work in many different ways, to suit their individual needs and talents. One can research, the other write and edit. They can both do the digging, then one compose and the other revise. Or they can do every step of the project together. As with ghosting, the arrangement can be whatever you agree on.

When law partners Colleen Cowles and Anne Brown teamed up to write their legal column for *The Community Times* (Eau Claire, Wisconsin) they divvied up chores. First they developed a list of topics and culled from it the ideas they found most interesting. Then Cowles, a former English teacher, took responsibility for composing first drafts. "I would sit down on a weekend and write anywhere from one to five columns," she says. "I found it was easier to write a series at one time. Then Anne did the cleanup." The biggest challenge the duo faced was boiling down legalese into readable English. With both of them refining and rechecking, they kept their discussion accurate while snipping out technical jargon.

Food writers Michael and Jane Stern spend two to three months a year scouring the country together, seeking out good restaurants and selecting recipes from menus for their syndicated "A Taste of America" column. When they return home, they're ready to translate their experiences onto paper. "We have different ways of writing together," Jane Stern says. "We conceive columns together and we'll talk them out. Michael may do most of the writing and I'll edit. Then we'll do the final draft together. Or we may do the opposite. Michael works at the word processor and I work at the typewriter, so Michael gets to type the final draft and put in the final editing."

Although many collaborators don't have contracts with each other, most think it's a good idea. Putting together an agreement, whether written or verbal, makes you think ahead about how you'll set up bylines and split fees, responsibilities, and liabilities.

Because collaborators work so closely, the relationship is a lot like marriage. To be successful, the partners should complement each other, share common areas of writing interest, have a healthy respect for each other's opinions and abilities, and be willing to compromise when necessary. Each must make a commitment to the partnership. Trust is essential; remember that your reputation will be tied to your partner's.

How do you find that perfect someone to team up with? First decide why you want a collaborator and what qualities you want in one. Consider work habits, writing style, knowledge, personality, ability to compromise, creativity, talent, etc. Again, if you're a writer with an idea but need an authoritative backup, professional associations, universities, and the like are where you should begin searching for a partner. On the other hand, experts without publication experience as well as writers seeking a comrade-in-ink can look to writers' organizations, writing courses, and local publications for collaborators.

Once you've found a potential partner, try writing a few sample columns together to see if your styles, work habits, and schedules mesh. For example, if ideas are your forte but your sentences tend to run on and you can never figure out where to put that comma or semicolon, then you'll need a partner to pare your verbosity and put the punctuation in place. But if your would-be collaborator doesn't know a colon from a semi and tends toward meandering prose, then what have you gained? If you have a positive answer to the question, then invest in a grammar book and be on your collaborative way.

3
Writing the Column

New columnists learn to find voice, style, and tone through trial and error—sharpening their observation skills, testing assorted literary devices, and trying out different ways of expressing themselves. In this chapter, we'll present the elements of good column writing, along with examples from successful columns.

How to Make a Point in a Few Words

A columnist must be a sharpshooter, firing each word directly toward the purpose each installment serves. No digressions,

verbosity, weak words, ineffectual phrases, or murky prose are
welcome in this type of writing.

> *"Reporters immerse themselves in infinite trivial de-
> tails day after day. A columnist sits back and contem-
> plates and thinks about how things work. . . . Reporting is
> purely a high speed matter of getting the quote. Colum-
> nists are ponderers. A columnist has the opportunity, if
> not the necessity, of being a writer, paying attention to
> prose."—Fred Reed,* Washington Times *science and soldier-
> ing columnist.*

In narrative features, all words focus to express a single idea,
following a logical, orderly progression. Other kinds of formats, too, require economy of words. "Dear Abby" must give
advice on a complex personal problem in two column inches
or so; catalogue columns must sell a product in a few sentences. No matter what the format, as gardening writer Doc
Abraham likes to say, "Keep it short and sweet and full of
meat." Below are some tips to cook up a piece according to
that flavorful formula.

Know what you want to say before putting pen to paper.
With only several hundred words to work with, you must
come up with a single well-defined slant. As former *Washington Post* commentator Roger Rosenblatt says, "It's important
for a column to look like a direct flight."

Suppose you want to do a column on the new criteria your
community has developed for screening foster parents. If your
objective is simply to inform readers of the changes, gather the
facts and present them. However, if you want readers to bom-
bard city officials with letters urging still stronger regulations,
then concentrate on presenting a convincing argument; don't
meander off into diatribe against departmental expenditures
for furniture.

> *"It takes your best skills as a journalist to take a techni-
> cal subject and explain it in plain English."—Bob Schwa-
> bach, syndicated computer columnist.*

"Stories have power. You can tell a story in two hundred pages or in 750 words. Just stick with the story; don't get off the point."—Mike Levine, political and social commentator for the Times Herald-Record *in Middletown, New York.*

Narrow your topic. If the subject encompasses a great amount of information, don't try to include everything in one column or you'll dilute the gist of your piece. Either weed out extraneous information or do a series of two or three installments.

Going back to the community foster care example, suppose you've discovered problems in your city's service and want to write about them. The physical living conditions of foster children might take up an entire day's space. Another day you could focus on the lack of supportive services available to these children and the families who have taken them in. A third column could discuss drug and alcohol abuse and a controversial new proposal to screen foster parents for these addictions. Cramming all these topics into one 800-word installment would make the piece merely a superficial accounting.

"Don't anticipate the news. You must comment on something that's universal knowledge. Otherwise you'll end up using the entire column to explain. Then when you get to the commentary part, where you're just turning the corner, you're out of space."—syndicated columnist Richard Cohen on writing commentary.

Consider your purpose and tone. Are you writing this particular installment to entertain? Inform? Motivate? A combination of these? The purpose of the column will affect the way you write it—the words you choose, the attitude you assume, the lengths of your sentences—and what information you include. For example, to amuse readers with tales of blunders on movie sets, you would not include the story of the staged car crash that crippled a stuntman. However, in a strictly informational piece, you might put that story in; in an investigative piece about abuses in filmmaking, you'd definitely use it.

Dave Barry on writing a humor column: "It's useful to have a good sense of humor, but, strangely enough, what is more important than that is technique. You must have the willingness to work on technique and to learn how to make a line sound funny. . . . The device I use most often is writing by indirection—leading the reader to think I'm going to say something and then saying something else."

In a column entertaining readers you have more latitude to play around with style, using clever metaphors, written sound effects, extensive description, for example, to set a light-hearted tone. But an investigative piece calls for a less showy display of writing. Style is still there, but it calls less attention to itself, so that literary acrobatics don't distract readers from the argument and facts. Therefore, decide ahead of time what you want to do and keep the tone consistent throughout the piece.

Decide how you'll make your point or convey your information. A column can be crafted in many different ways: as a single anecdote, a series of anecdotes, satire, an argument, a list of tips, instructions, a combination of these. Decide which is the most effective method for you, your column's format, and the subject matter, and the message, advice, or information you want to communicate. In the foster home example, you could illustrate the problem of lax screening by simply telling one little boy's story. Or you could use statistics, examples of inappropriate placements, interviews with social workers, or a satirical account of bureaucratic bungling.

Write a working headline. Don't worry about coming up with something catchy here. Just encapsulate your installment (for instance, "Safety Problems in Movie Stunts") in a simple statement, and refer to it as you write to keep the piece on track.

Plan an outline. Especially for a narrative column, organize your thoughts with an outline or list of salient points. No matter how informal, an outline is a useful tool and a good discipline, particularly for beginners. Once you've written a number of columns, you may, as some pros do, dispense with a written outline, mapping out the framework in your head instead.

Choose words carefully. Because a columnist has so little room to maneuver, the basic principles of good writing are especially important in putting together a column. The fundamental of all fine writing is "Show, don't tell." Fill the canvas of your column with vivid pictures. The stronger your images, the more your readers can "see" what you're talking about and the more they'll keep their eyes glued to the page.

Below are several pointers for focusing your writing to make it more lively. For an extensive discussion, we highly recommend Gary Provost's *Make Every Word Count*.

- *Use concrete nouns and specific adjectives.* Descriptive nouns and adjectives focus an image. *Station wagon* rather than *vehicle*. *Eighteen-wheeler* rather than *truck*. Avoid nondescript adjectives. A "pleasant" or a "nice" girl means what? On the other hand, *outgoing, perky,* and *well-mannered* give useful information. However, keep adjectives to a minimum. Too many lead to sensory overload and bog down the rhythm of a piece.
- *Use strong, active verbs.* Strong verbs are descriptive and specific. They have movement, a tangibility about them. They don't just lie there, waiting for an adverb to pull them along. For example, which gives a better picture: "The boy walked down the street," "The boy walked slowly down the street," or "The boy trudged down the street"? What about "They had an argument" versus "They argued"? Too many weak or passive verbs mute the colors of your prose. It's the difference between a friend's saying, "There's an exciting chase scene in the movie *Bullitt*," and your clutching your seat in the theatre as you watch Steve McQueen's car fly down the hilly streets of San Francisco.

"Clear punchy prose with a funny [humorous] turn of phrase will get you a long way."—Fred Reed, Washington Times *science and soldiering columnist.*

Watch out for excessive use of the verb *to be*. It slows the pace to a crawl, sapping the energy of a piece. *To be* in combination with a past participle turns the subject of a sentence into a passive receiver of the action. For example, unless you're specifically trying to show passivity in a person, avoid a string of sentences like this: The man was awakened. His socks and shoes were donned. The car was driven to the restaurant. He was met by a friend and was bought dinner.

• *Eliminate adverbs whenever possible.* Adverbs troop after weak verbs, propping them up and supplying them with definition. If you need an adverb to complete your image, your verb is probably shirking its duty.

• *Use short, familiar words.* They keep action moving at a rapid clip, while multisyllabic words slow a march down to a dirge. A simple sentence like "Dressed in our summer Sunday best, we strolled down the sidewalk and window shopped" becomes unpalatable when gussied up in a lot of $100 words: "Bedecked in all our Sunday finery, we perambulated along the pavement and ogled the merchandise in the retail establishments." Each sequined and bejeweled word shouts for attention like a stage full of prima donnas.

The Lead

The recipe for an effective narrative column is a strong lead to hook readers in, a meaty middle to feed their interest, and a solid ending to send them on their way, mulling over an argument, smiling at a zany adventure, stoked up to see a movie. But, no matter how exciting the middle or end, if the first few lines don't grab readers, they won't stay around to see what follows. Even in a Q&A, placing the most intriguing question first piques interest.

Admittedly, coming up with consistently snappy leads can be a challenge. Even the best scribes have off days. However, because of their high batting average, fans allow them an occasional strikeout. But, for new writers, reputations rely on a strong performance in their initial at-bats.

While there's no magic formula for ingenuity, here are a few pointers for strong openings.

Make readers care. If readers have an emotional stake in a subject, they'll want to read straight through. To get them involved, start with the human element—people's actions, emotions, likes, dislikes, frustrations, experiences. Even if you're discussing science, weather, stocks and bonds, or photography, bring in the human touch by either starting off with a short anecdote or bringing the reader directly into the story. Look at soldiering columnist Fred Reed's lead to a piece on flying in an F-15, which appeared in *The Washington Times*.

> Maybe you think flying a fighter plane is exhilarating or thrilling—swooping, climbing, diving, soaring through the clouds in graceful curves just like Jonathan Livingston Seagull. Hah! Actually, it is more like throwing up in a wetsuit while being run over by several trucks simultaneously. In particular, a dogfight is not what the movies would have you believe.

Right off, Reed lifts us to the skies. The active verbs take us cavorting through the heavens with him. First he plays into our preconceived pictures of flying. Then he pulls us into a stall and sends us into a tailspin by vividly describing the reality, putting it into terms we can all imagine. In giving readers something to identify with, he has taken a technical subject with limited appeal and made it interesting to a general readership.

Appealing to readers' self-interest can also capture an audience. For example, a home-repair column on purchasing and maintaining a new kitchen floor might begin: "Do you know that many 'easy maintenance' no-wax floors may cost you hours on your knees? If you'd rather confine your workouts to aerobics, here's what to consider when you're buying a floor." Of course, anyone buying an easy-to-clean floor wants to know how much time he or she will have to spend cleaning it, and our columnist lures readers in with an offer to help them make the right decision.

Make a promise and keep it. A good grab 'em lead makes an implicit promise. From the first few sentences, readers should know what to expect from a column—will they be informed? entertained? moved? given a peek behind a curtain? The promise can be stated overtly, as in the home-repair column on floors. Or it can be conveyed in the way you create a tone, scene, or mood. Look at this lead by syndicated columnist Roger Simon.

> It was raining.
> Gray clouds loped across the sky like dirty sheep. The wind blew through the concrete canyons of downtown and spit in my face.
> I tightened the belt on my trench coat and leaned up against the phone booth waiting for the Chief to call.
> I lit a cigar. That was breakfast. The most important meal of the day.

From the first outlandish image of clouds lumbering across the sky like dirty sheep, we know we're in for a humorous story. The short, clipped sentences parody Raymond Chandler's detective novels and hint at witty entertainment, which Simon then delivers as he satirizes undercover news gathering.

> *"Provoke people to think, but not necessarily the way you do."—Mike Levine, political and social commentator for the* Times Herald-Record *in Middletown, New York.*

Make a strong statement. Lead off with a controversial statement, a strong opinion, or a shocker to arouse readers. For instance, when Middletown, (N.Y) *Times Herald-Record* commentator Mike Levine writes: "Tomorrow is Veterans Day, a day of national honor. In Orange County, it will be a day of shame," people in Orange County will want to know what they've done wrong, and they'll keep reading this column about a legislature that would not commit a small sum to build a memorial honoring local citizens who died in Vietnam.

Appeal to the senses. Sight, sound, taste, smell, touch words enliven prose. Good travel, food, and restaurant writers, especially, use sensory description to invite readers to savor experiences along with them, as in this lead by food writers Jane and Michael Stern, beckoning readers into Sam's Grill:

> Enter through old-fashioned saloon doors and you are guided to a high-walled private booth. Pull back the curtain, and there is your table, draped with a starchy white cloth. On the cloth is a loaf of outstanding brittle-crusted sourdough bread.

Is your mouth watering for the sourdough bread? Can you feel it break in your hands and hear the crunch of the crust tearing? After this tantalizing lead, the Sterns continue to draw readers in, paragraph after paragraph, with additional concrete, sensory images.

Paint vivid pictures. Sometimes images alone pull readers in. Just as a Picasso canvas might cause us to pause and reflect over it, so may a writer's use of color, line, or juxtaposition of elements in the beginning paragraphs of a column lure readers. Syndicated columnist Ellen Goodman's lead for a feature using the plight of a stranded whale as a metaphor for Soviet-U.S. communication illustrates the effective use of active verbs, concrete pictures, and clever setup of seemingly disparate images to make us read on. Look how she stirs us with commands, grabbing us by the lapels, and drawing us into the column, delighting us with the wit of her vision.

> Put aside your summit scorecards; take down the pinups of Gorbachev and Reagan; stop counting "us and them" missiles for a minute. Let's hear it for Humphrey the Humpback Whale.

To Do: Choose several columnists you admire and clip three columns from each writer. Look at the leads. Are they effective? What techniques did the writers use to make them so? If a lead didn't work, how can it be improved? Pretend you're the columnist and rewrite the lead, sprucing it up if you can. Use active verbs, specific nouns, simple words. Include the five senses, if applicable.

To Do: Now go back to the mock columns you sketched out in the last chapter. Write a lead, keeping the tips we've given you in mind. Then go on and make your point, detail your instructions, or convey your information using the appropriate format section of Chapter Two as a guideline. (Q&A columnists should concentrate on starting with an interesting question and writing a strong answer.) Hold off writing the conclusion until you've read the next section.

The Ending

Unlike news stories, which are written so that the last few paragraphs can be lopped off to fit available space, most columns must have a definite finish. In wrapping up, sometimes the words come to a natural halt, but more often than not, the writer has to work at concluding the piece gracefully. Here are some closing devices that have been used successfully over the years.

Tie-in with the lead. Repeating key words or phrases from the lead in the finale of a column brings a feature full circle. Look at the beginning of *The* (Baltimore) *Sun* writer Isaac Rehert's piece, "A Country Boy of the Old School":

> He was a country boy of the old school, still unacquainted with the artificialities of life. He came, he saw, he fell in love with a woolly white ram. And he swapped his enthusiasm, his sweat and those simple skills that even a slip of a country boy acquires before he is half grown to take home with him the object of his aspirations.

The column goes on to talk about the boy's fascination with Rehert's rams and how the writer gives the youth one of the animals in exchange for fixing the fence.

Now read Rehert's ending, with its repetition of the word *country* and the phrase "country boy of the old school," as he ties in the boy's simple values and willingness to barter to his own (Rehert's) fears that progress will bring this neighborly commerce to an end:

> I hope that naive quality of his will be one the world he will grow up to will reward. I have apprehensions. For he is just a country boy of the old school. And the country is filling up with prosperous cities—with factories where the worker punches the clock, and the computer counts his hours and calculates to the penny how much he has earned; and with supermarkets, where they proclaim unmistakably the price of every item that's for sale.
>
> I hope there is a place in those cities where the naive country boys can prosper too.

Another way to tie in with your lead is to leave readers with vivid images that amplify the general points you've addressed in your lead. Cathy Johnson used this device in one of her "Cathy's Corner" columns in the monthly *Newsletter of Parenting*. She starts off talking about two-year-olds' penchant for orderliness and predictability and concludes with these strong pictures of how her own toddler exemplifies this state:

> So we know we're in for a crisis of major proportions if we allow the Rice Krispies to run out. So we face tears and screams if a cautious adult attempts to move her juice glass out of a direct line between milk pitcher and cereal bowl, where she has carefully positioned it. So she believes that watching "Dangermouse" on TV follows bathtime as the night the day. It's not such a big price to pay, considering the benefits.

Anecdote. Similarly, you can end with an anecdote that illustrates an argument or reinforces a point. Or use a story to round out a personality piece or provoke thought. Ginger Hutton, an *Arizona Republic* columnist, placed this anecdote at the end of a piece on vanity license plate watching:

> Fred Hillegas, retired KTAR radio announcer, told of seeing an interesting juxtaposition of plates.
> "Call this to each his/her own," he said. "Near my home one day I saw a car with plates that said 1 4 GOD. A few minutes later, in the parking lot of a nearby shopping center, I saw another car with plates saying 2 4 FUN."

Or begin a column with the first part of an anecdote and wind up the feature with the story's conclusion and you've built suspense. Columnist Paul Berg of *The Washington Post* does this in one segment of a bits-and-pieces column on health care. He begins:

> A California woman, claiming bruises she suffered in a traffic accident caused her to develop breast cancer, last week was awarded more than $600,000 in damages.

In the middle of the item, Berg reports that experts have not linked traumatic injury with causing cancer. He concludes his piece with the end of the anecdote—a real surprise:

> In the California case, doctors testified that the cancer developed on the exact place where Pamela Rock, 32, of Anaheim Hills, was bruised by her steering wheel in the accident, and that breast cancer rarely appears in such a position on the breast.
> She had a double mastectomy. According to court records, there was a history of cancer in her family.

Summary. In summing up, a writer restates the purpose of the column and pulls all arguments, points, and facts together. This device is especially effective in how-to and other service pieces, where the writer can reiterate advice to close a column. In their "Making Sense of the Law" column for *The Community Times* of Eau Claire, Wisconsin, lawyers Anne Brown and Colleen Cowles employed this technique to conclude an

installment discussing the implications of the new Wisconsin
Marital Property Act:

> Due to the broad effect of the Wisconsin Marital Property
> Act on estate planning, between now and Jan. 1, 1986
> would be a wise time to reassess your estate plan to deter-
> mine whether it meets your needs and desires. Remember,
> everyone has an estate plan. The question is, is it the plan of
> your choice, or has the state designated your estate plan
> because you have not? Do you know what would happen
> to your property and to your loved ones? If not, or if you are
> unsure of how the new law will effect your estate plan, you
> should find out before Jan. 1, 1986.

Recipe or list ending. Lists, recipes, or hints at the end of a
column can supplement or highlight material discussed in the
body of a piece. Dee Hardie, columnist for *House Beautiful*,
wrote a mouth-watering reminiscence extolling her father's
clam chowder, telling how he would don his white apron every Fourth of July and brew up a kettle of the creamy soup. The
column ends just the way the reader hopes—with the
treasured family recipe. Singles columnist Stephen Atlas finished an installment on seeking supportive friends when a
spouse dies with a checklist of advice on coping with the grief.
Chef Louis Szathmary often concludes his food columns with
shopping hints and tips on choosing a wine.

> *"Quotes make a column more lively, more human,
> more personal."—Charles Salter, fishing and weather col-
> umnist for the Atlanta* Constitution.

Quotations. Sometimes a quote captured during an interview
wraps up a column in a neat package, summing up a feeling or
giving readers more to ponder. In a *Columbia* (Maryland) *Flier* column detailing a father's agony over the murder of his
fourteen-year-old daughter, writer Ramsey Flynn ends with
the parent's plea to the community to do more about missing
children. The quote gives additional impact to the piece:

> "I'm not saying the whole force should drop everything
> to go out and find runaways," says Brittingham, "but we
> need to look at some changes. . . . We need priorities, and
> one of our first priorities is our greatest natural resource for
> the future, our kids."

In addition, writers sometimes close their columns with a famous quotation or adage. If you use one of these endings, make sure it supports a specific purpose or effect: otherwise, it will sound tacked on and subtract from your piece rather than add to it. In a humorous treatise on the arbitrary length of women's skirts, syndicated columnist Ellen Goodman gets in some shots at designers who forget that real women must wear their creations. She closes her commentary with a take-off on fashion writers' hype, including the standard reporter's tag line:

> Now they [designers] have presented us with the su-
> preme challenge. The true elegante, the fashionable wom-
> an of 1980, will be the person who changes her height to
> go with her outfit. Tall by day, short by night (or vice versa),
> she will be unfettered, liberated from the old archaic limits
> of mere inches. Hosanna.
> Just remember . . . you read it here first.

The shocker. Close with an unexpected statement that jolts readers. Canadian writer June Callwood's column on the invasion of Grenada in the *Globe and Mail* discusses the events leading to the military action and its aftermath. She begins by talking about the lovely summer weather in Canada and how far away citizens of that northern country are from the sounds of pain and war issuing from the beleaguered Caribbean island. The writer then details the plight of political prisoners there: the beatings, the isolation, the ill health, the lack of legal counsel. At the end of 900 words on war and despair, Callwood concludes: "Such a gentle summer. Here."

Question. Question endings can provoke thought, motivate readers, or reinforce the general tone of a piece. For example, in a column on New York District Attorney Robert Morganthau's attempts to indict Bernhard Goetz, the New York City subway vigilante who shot four would-be assailants, syndicated writer Jeffrey Hart examines Morganthau's actions. The columnist wraps up the piece with a question asking whose side Mr. Morganthau is really on—the political establishment's or the people's.

Obviously, if you're doing a bits-and-pieces or a question-and-answer column, you don't usually have to worry about finding the perfect finale. However, each segment in itself needs a logical close. How-to pieces also fall into this category. In many cases the last step or a comment on the object's utility or beauty can round off the piece.

To Do: Write an ending to your column, choosing one of the devices we've listed above. Then try a second and third device. Familiarize yourself with the different ways of finishing a piece so that each method becomes a natural part of your repertoire.

Picking a Point of View

Another important style consideration is point of view. Are you, the writer, going to step to center stage and be an actor in your column? Or will you function as director and control the column from behind the scenes?

Choosing the former role means writing in first person, using *I* or *we* to reinforce your presence or authority. First person is a natural choice for many columnists. Because the *I* point of view allows opinion and highlights a writer's personality, Andy Rooney, Mike Royko, William Safire, and many others employ it.

Note, too, that sometimes the *I* is implied, as it is by many commentary writers when they're expressing an opinion but don't want the *I* to distract from their arguments. For example, in an October 5, 1985 column published in the Columbus *Citizen-Journal,* syndicated columnist Julian Bond wrote about a survey of black civil rights leaders ". . . do Lichter's results argue for wholesale resignations among black leaders and a turning away from the positions held by civil-rights leaders for a generation? That seems to be the effect of the Lichter study, if not the intent." Although Bond hasn't come right out and said "I think," his statement leads us to understand that this conclusion about the effect of the report reflects his own interpretation and opinion.

Any column that offers an opinion, whether a review, how-to, consumer feature, or whatever, can be done in the first person if personalizing it is your intention. The *I* form puts an individual behind the advice or critique. The reader, therefore, feels as though he or she is taking part in a private conversation with you.

If you don't want to stand in the spotlight, second or third person will convey your message without shouting "here I am" to the reader. Second person, speaking to the audience using *you* or an implied *you*, works well for recipes and how-to's. The imperative form keeps distractions to a minimum.

Use third person, *he*, *she*, *it*, or *they*, when not directly addressing readers. Whenever you want a reportorial effect to convey information without opinion, third person lets you step out of the picture so the story tells itself. For example, a columnist who would like to show the world through the eyes of unemployed high school dropouts must let the subjects speak for themselves.

A columnist may do all writing in one person or may use different viewpoints. After beginning a real estate column with a first-person opinion on the market, the writer might follow with tips (second person) on how to make a house more saleable. Or on a Monday a social commentator might write a first-person essay on the joys of eating chocolate, and on Wednesday present a third-person account of a battered child's first four years of life. Which viewpoint you employ is a style decision based on your subject, the mood you want to create, how close you want to get to your audience at that moment, and how much you want to be part of that story.

"If the column works, it shouldn't sound like writing. You want people to think 'that's a good story.' "—Mike Levine, political and social commentator for the Times Herald-Record *in Middletown, New York.*

Using a Persona

A special form of point of view is speaking through a persona, an assumed identity or facade adopted for the purposes of the column, like an actor's taking on a role. A persona allows a writer to step beyond the bounds of his or her own personality and embrace the characteristics, attitudes, and opinions of a fictional speaker to set a tone or hit home a point.

A classic example of a writer who assumes a persona is Art Buchwald. His naive persona acts as a foil for the author's satirical comments on politics and society. Buchwald the columnist obviously knows the score. For instance, although he knows that no political candidate really has a monopoly on God's support, he devotes an entire column to an interview by his naive character with the Almighty about this issue. By virtue of his innocence, the persona can take on public personages, reducing their rationalizations for their actions to absurdity by his guileless interrogatories. Sometimes the columnist does a switch, having an astute character do the querying while the persona defends a position with ludicrous reasoning. Either way, Buchwald makes his point effectively.

A persona should never be forced; it should sound as if it comes naturally. To use a persona successfully, the writer should have some of the skills of a novelist. A columnist must crawl inside the character and see the world through the character's eyes. While the persona needn't be 100 percent flesh and blood to the reader, it must remain consistent with itself. It can't be naive one sentence and all-knowing the next.

If you're planning to try out a persona, it's best to attempt it when the stakes are low—for example, when you're writing for a small circulation paper, says Ramsey Flynn, who served his apprenticeship at several little newspapers before becoming a senior writer at a city magazine. "It's like an off-off Broadway experiment," he says. In small publications you're freer to try out new roles. "And it's nice to be able to do that on a small stage. If you do it on a big stage, you just might be afraid to go out and try it again."

Not every kind of column lends itself to a persona. Most won't. However, before you erase the idea from your mind, think again. Who would have dreamt that a subject like etiquette would lend itself to this technique? Yet, look at Miss Manners who dispenses serious advice mixed with satire. Miss M. sometimes does pontificate from on high. But because we know that Judith Martin's behind it with her tongue placed firmly in cheek, we let her get away with it, laughing at her snooty insistence on oh-so-proper behavior yet considering her advice.

> *"Writers' standards aren't high enough. They don't read enough of what's been written or can't tell what's good. 'I spent a lot of time on this,' they tell themselves, 'so it must be good.' Well, you can almost always make it better. . . . Writing is selling. More often than not what you're selling isn't as good as it should be."—Dave Barry, humor columnist.*

Revision

Revision smooths the rough spots, preparing a column for its appearance before its audience. In initial drafts, most columnists scramble to get information and thoughts down, not worrying about syntax, spelling, or style. Then during subsequent drafts—the number depends on the writer and the subject—authors concentrate on nuances, ordering ideas logically, cleaning up grammar, spicing up verbs, cutting out the extraneous, expanding important points, and pepping up prose. In a column, where words can't be wasted, it's a rare writer who can do all of the above on the first try. Even for a pro like Art Buchwald, revision is a fact of life. "I do a draft and keep honing it down and honing it down so that it gets shaped up and I don't waste any words," he says.

Let time elapse between a draft and its revision—even if it's only a matter of an hour or so. After the break, you can come back with distance and a fresh perspective. More than likely, the respite will enable you to tackle the column with renewed vigor.

To Do: Since you're just beginning your career as a columnist and have been working on your feature for the last three chapters, we suggest you take a day or two away from your feature. Then pull it out and see how it reads. Check your writing against the tips in "Choose Words Carefully" on pages 39-40. Also, check grammar and spelling. Have you backed up opinions or assertions you've made with strong supports (facts, stories, statistics)? If you're presenting an argument, is it logical? Have you thought out your position, put your emotions aside, and presented a strong appeal for your point of view? If you're doing a how-to piece, have you listed all the steps, and are they in order? Have you listed all the materials?

A Pro's Prose

Now that you've learned some of the techniques of writing a column, take a look at them in the hands of a pro, Roger Rosenblatt, in "Revenge My Sweet," a column written for *The Washington Post*:

People of feeble or damaged character are prone to seek revenge for wrongs done them, or so it is necessary to tell me, for I have always believed that vengeance is the Lord's.

Even after that unpleasantness at Wolfie's, I believed it—even after lying like a suicidal turtle on the motel bed, rigid with pain on my ruptured disc, and speaking into the phone out of the side of my grimace as if I were a spaceman taking off, trying all the while to sound powerful, rational:

But Mr. Wolf (I told the owner), the doctor says I ought not to be'moved for another day.

But Mr. Rosenblatt, I promised your room to a man from Canada.

But Mr. Wolf, you can give the man from Canada another room, until I'm gone.

But Mr. Rosenblatt, I promised your room to a man from Canada.

But Mr. Wolf, I'd like to rip this phone off the wall and shove it in your eye.

Outside I heard Florida and the whooping bathers, and then the ambulance that had arrived to round off my halcyon vacation with a nine-day stretch in the hospital, there to dream drugged dreams of wolf slaughter, of the dumb, fat-headed chief of wolves being dragged by ambulance on his back through the bleached avenues of Cocoa Beach, while men from Canada jeered from the sidelines.

But those were unworthy dreams. And soon I regained my former virtue, trusting in divine providence to do whatever divine providence does in such matters. There was nothing I could do on my own anyway. Write a vilifying essay? Never write to get even. Sue him? I wouldn't know how. Live well—supposedly the best revenge? Out of the question. Kill him? Perhaps. But the giant wooden sign outside Wolfie's was in the shape of a Little Red Riding Hood wolf with teeth the size of toasters, and if the sign were a true likeness of my enemy, there'd be no killing Wolf. So I arose from my hospital bed, and quit Cocoa Beach, bearing only the noble thoughts for which I am universally known.

Not that revenge can't be noble too, of course. The Elizabethan playwrights wrote "revenge tragedies" in which some very low things were done by some very high people. In John Webster's "Dutchess of Malfi," for example, the dutchess marries the forbidden Antonio, flees, is betrayed by her servant, Bosola, then is captured by her brothers Ferdinand and the cardinal, tortured, and finally strangled, along with her two children. But then Bosola kills the cardinal, Ferdinand kills Bosola, and Ferdinand goes mad; so it all works out.

Then there's the lovely Greek story of Prince Tereus who marries Procne and fathers Itys, a son. One day, with time on his hands, Tereus summons Procne's sister Philomela from Athens on the pretext that Procne is dead, then ravishes Philomela in the woods, and cuts out her tongue, in spite of which Philomela manages to tell Procne what happened, and the two sisters serve Itys to Tereus for dinner, after which the gods take revenge on the whole crew, and change them all into birds.

And "Hamlet" is a tale of revenge; as is "Macbeth"; as in our own day is "The Abominable Dr. Phibes," in which Vincent Price, seeking vengeance for his wife's death, recreates the plagues of "Exodus," such as the frog mask that fits snugly over his victim's head, and then decreases steadily in size.

Yet these are stories of great wrongs greatly righted; whereas in my experience it is the smallest offense that boils the blood. Hurl a grenade at my car, and I may yell. But give the slightest casual injury to my youthful vanity or sense of justice and I will see you hanging upside down, disemboweled, from Mt. Whitney, your hair aflame, your body coated with rabid bees.

But, naturally, I use "I" in the abstract, being one of those who upon injury seek nothing but guidance. Which is why I felt only remorse and piety last week, when I picked up the papers and read that a totally unexpected tornado had hit the city of Cocoa Beach, Florida, miraculously killing no one, yet knocking the daylights out of a motel called Wolfie's.

Thy will be done.

In the lead, the passive *to be* sets the tone and clues us into his feelings. A victim of an insensitive motel owner who kicks him out of his room despite his debilitating pain, Rosenblatt employs the passive voice, underscoring his helplessness. He asks for our sympathy, encouraging us to root for him, the underdog.

In paragraphs two through six, the author opens each sentence with the refrain, "But, Mr . . ." as he pleads with the unyielding Mr. Wolf. The repetition of the phrase by sound and rhythm reinforces a picture of two people butting heads.

Next, Rosenblatt is hauled off to a hospital, where none of us would want to spend our vacation, and wallows in vivid dreams of revenge. Note the concrete punishments his imagination cooks up to get even. How much better than simply telling us "I was angry."

Alas, revenge is not to be his. But that doesn't stop our narrator from discoursing on some of the literary high points of getting even. This catalogue of crime and punishment provides a respite from the reader's anger at Mr. Wolf while justifying the victim's right to feel vengeful. The next to the last long paragraph brings the piece back to the present and ends with the narrator's blow-by-blow description, complete with concrete pictures such as "body coated with rabid bees," of the fitting punishment for those who wrong him. Once again, Rosenblatt uses strong images to stoke the reader's feelings.

After all the colorful talk of revenge, the last paragraph starts out calmly, with the author's adopting a reasonable tone. Then he casually drops the bombshell—Wolfie's has been blown to smithereens by a tornado.

The simple, familiar quotation, "Thy will be done," provides a fitting conclusion, and we can almost see Rosenblatt sitting back piously with his hands folded. A higher power has stepped in and dealt a blow to the callous Mr. Wolf. Divine retribution does indeed exist.

4
The Ongoing Column

Columnists have the unique opportunity to establish a long-term relationship with their readers. In this chapter we'll discuss how to develop a faithful following and how to come up with material to sustain readers' attention.

Establishing Rapport

Just as folks who see each other frequently and enjoy each other's company form an attachment, so do columnist and reader form a bond. In this kind of "friendship," however, the burden of establishing the rapport falls to the writer. "The key to a successful column is to start to involve your reading public," says

57

George Hamersley, former community columnist for *The* (Ocean City-Somers Point, N.J.) *Record*. "The way to do this is to get the tempo of the congregation—the pulse of the reading public. You've got to play to them."

Good columns speak directly to the reader. They cajole, exhort, praise, inform, entertain, motivate, stir emotions. A skilled columnist never writes at readers; he or she talks to them and with them. Each writer has a method of getting close to an audience. Below we've listed some techniques.

Visualize your reader. Many columnists picture a particular person when they sit down to write their columns. Heloise, who took over her late mother's household hints column, wrote her first installment under the older woman's tutelage. As the daughter nervously anticipated putting down her first words in black and white, the elder Heloise offered, of course, a helpful hint. "Sit down and write this as if you're talking to your best friend, Ann." Today Heloise II still imagines she's chatting with Ann as she puts together each installment of tips. "I'm talking to her, not lecturing or writing at her," the columnist says. "I'm not writing a textbook; I'm talking to a real person."

"I think of an old lady sitting on a porch, or an invalid just having a lonely time of it," says Mike Levine, opinion columnist, assistant editor, and writing coach for the Middletown (N.Y.) *Times Herald-Record*. "I feel I'm a connection to someone. I use this sometimes to goad myself if I'm having trouble with a paragraph. Will this make sense to that person? Am I communicating or just playing with words? That imaginary person is a check off for me."

House Beautiful's Dee Hardie, whose mailbox is crammed with notes from devoted fans, says, "Because of the letters I receive, I know my audience. People say that reading my column is like getting a letter from a friend every month." To keep her tone conversational, the author talks aloud as she writes, transposing the rhythms of her speech to print.

To Consider: Visualize your target audience. How would you talk to them if you were holding a conversation? Or pick out an individual, real or imaginary. Again, how would you talk to him or her? Think about this as you go on to read the rest of this section.

Personalize your delivery. Let your personality shine through. Columnist Ann Landers's success is due not only to the practical advice she gives but also to her trademark personal delivery. If she thinks a reader deserves a pat on the back for having coped with a difficult situation, she reaches out in print and touches that person's shoulder. If a reader is agonizing over whether to leave an abusive husband, Landers fires off her stock question, "Would you be better off without him?" If she thinks a fan is off-target, she sets the reader straight with her famous line, "Wake up and smell the coffee." Landers goes out on a limb and infuses the column with her warm, but no-nonsense, personality.

> *"I never did trust a fellow who wouldn't look me in the eye, so I always try to maintain eye contact when I'm interviewing. It's important to prove your sincerity to the people you're writing about. Be yourself. Be friendly."*— *Charles Salter, fishing and weather columnist for the At-lanta* Constitution.

No matter what kind of column you do, be yourself, not a carbon copy of someone else. No one can be Erma Bombeck better than she can. William F. Buckley has years of practice being William F. Buckley, and no upstart could play the role as well. If you want to capture a readership, don't force your writing into someone else's mold; let your style flow from your own personality.

Give something of yourself. If your subject permits, inject bits of information about yourself to let readers feel there's a human being behind the words.

Ann Landers's in-print disclosure of her failed marriage and impending divorce several years ago brought her closer to her audience. Her willingness to open up to readers, as they had to her, endeared Landers to them; they could empathize with her problems as she had done with theirs.

You may not want to put yourself into every installment, but an occasional glimpse into you and your life strengthens the reader-writer bond. For example, every now and then Richard Cohen slips in a personal piece amid his columns on national politics, social issues, and international diplomacy. He gives us ringside seats as he battles bats in his bathroom, wrestles with his cigarette habit, struggles with an unproductive day, offering insight into Cohen the person while providing illustrations for his social commentary.

Start a dialogue. Inviting and encouraging readers to take part in a dialogue atuomatically sets up a mechanism to keep them involved, and it can make the difference between a one-dimensional column and a spirited exchange that readers have a stake in. For instance, not only do fans write Ann Landers for advice, but they also send inspirational poems and tips, which she prints. Nor are they shy about letting her know when they agree or disagree with one of her answers.

> *"Give the column conversation instead of monologue."—Mike Levine, political and social commentator for the* Times Herald-Record *in Middletown, New York.*

Several Baltimore *Evening Sun* columnists, such as essayist Elise Chisolm, personalities writer Stephanie, and computer columnist Michael J. Himowitz, list their office telephone numbers and the hours they're available at the end of their columns. By talking to readers, they find out what people are thinking and what's happening in the community.

Obviously, not all columns lend themselves to this kind of audience participation, but it's something to consider. Why not do a movie column where once a week readers get to give their opinions on films showing at the local cinema? Or a sports feature where readers nominate a player of the week, with a line or two supporting their vote? Or a travel column in which people share good and bad experiences?

Don't talk down to readers. Assuming a condescending tone immediately sets up a barrier between writer and reader. In a nutrition column, an "eat your green beans, it's for your own good" stance doesn't work nearly as well as a "green beans are good for all of us" posture. A nonjudgmental or positive attitude toward the mental capacity, ability, knowledge, and taste of readers goes a lot farther in endearing you to them.

Syndicated newspaper columnist Bob Schwabach, who boils down the complexities of computers for a general audience, says, "I always remember my readers are as sharp as I am. They just don't know this particular area. I assume they are interested in computers and have some minimal knowledge, and I assume that people who know a lot will go to read more technical journals."

"You must be very specific when writing instructions. Don't assume anything."—Heloise, syndicated household hints columnist.

"You've got to remember to do the very best you can on every column. You can say, 'Oh, I've just got to get the copy done. It's just one issue.' But you never know who will see that column and depend upon it."—Heloise, syndicated household hints columnist.

Establish authority and trust. Readers will give up on a columnist who doesn't level with them. As we noted earlier, they have a right to expect that information they get from a column is accurate. Even political opinion columnists must have their facts straight, regardless of their interpretations.

Be prepared to go the extra mile to gather facts and to make sure your sources are trustworthy and accurate. For instance, Heloise doesn't simply print the household hints her readers send in. "Something [a hint] that seems very simple to work can cause a problem or be damaging," she points out. That's why every tip that goes into "Hints From Heloise" gets checked out by her or her staff. "If it goes in my column, I've tested it, or I've written about it before so I know it works or my secretary has tried it out." In addition, the columnist spends hours on the phone calling laboratories, manufacturers, county extension services, and other sources to corroborate hints or answer readers' queries.

Getting Ideas

Once you've signed on with a publication, you'll face the challenge of filling that space week after week, month after month. At first, ideas may flow freely, but what happens a year or two down the road? How do you keep coming up with topics to fill the expanse looming beneath your byline?

Some writers claim that ideas jump out at them from behind every bush, billboard, and building. They learn to keep an open mind, alert for possibilities in everything they read, see, or do. As Newark (N.J.) *Star-Ledger* environmental columnist Gordon Bishop puts it "You never turn off. You're always on. I'm taking a shower, I'm mowing the lawn, and I'm thinking about the column."

Other columnists, especially those with more narrowly defined subject matter, may discover that, after a while, the quest for new material is tougher than finding items on a scavenger hunt. Listed below are some sources writers tap for inspiration. Read through them and see which you can use to supply the seeds for ideas for your columns.

One's own store of experience. Many writers take topics from their everyday lives. If your car breaks down in the middle of a six-lane freeway, write about it. If you try skydiving, put it on paper. Roger Rosenblatt's "Revenge My Sweet" exemplifies this. He took a bad back and insensitive motel owner and turned the situation into a delightful reading experience.

Life around you. Columnists stay alert to what's happening around them. George Hamersley, whose community bits-and-pieces feature gave a capsule view of life at a New Jersey shore resort, found that strolling down the boardwalk or roaming through town and chatting with people gave him columns' worth of material. Gannett Westchester-Rockland newspapers' sports columnist Richard Gutwillig points out that the mark of a good writer is keeping one's eyes open to all the possibilities. "If you go to cover a game and can't come up with a game story, a feature, and a column, then you're not paying attention," he declares.

"The idea is to listen," says Mike Levine of the Middletown *Times Herald-Record*. "If a dozen people are in a drugstore, there are twelve columns. You have to have the ability to make connections from the specific to the general or from the general to the specific." In other words, when you have a long wait in a doctor's office, generalize from your personal experience, betting that most readers have found themselves in similar circumstances and will identify with your grumblings. Going from general to specific, for example, would be deciding to do a column on alcoholism among preteens and then devoting the column to the story of one eleven-year-old who has been hooked (disguising his identity, of course).

Other people. Readers, friends, people in the community, and relatives feed columnists ideas—some good, some atrocious. Columnists quickly learn to separate the wheat from the chaff. And there will be a lot of chaff. However, what at first seems a bad topic may lead to a workable one.

Syndicated columnist Roger Simon says, "Ideas come to me from all over: what I hear, what I think, what I see, what I feel, what I report on, what people tell me, what people phone in, what colleagues tell me. Sometimes ideas come directly from readers." For example, on the fortieth anniversary of the bombings of Hiroshima and Nagasaki, a reader called to say that the attacks had to be looked at in the context of the times, remembering there was a war on. The columnist still wasn't convinced the subject merited a day's space. Not until a second caller echoed the first, and after some thought, did Simon do a column. In response, thousands of letters poured in from people saying that they, too, felt the bombings had been justified. "However," the writer points out, "most columns don't come this way. Of one hundred calls, ninety-eight won't result in a column."

A network. In addition to using ideas that just happen your way, you can consider developing a roster of contact people who feed you news and information about your field. For example, Barry Garron, television and radio critic for the *Kansas City Star*, has developed sources and contacts at virtually every TV and radio station in his area. During his rookie season, he took the initiative, calling them, introducing himself, and asking for tips and information. Now that a rapport has developed, they frequently phone him. Having sources he can count on keeps him on top of his field.

Editors. Editors often hand staff columnists possible topics. Sports columnist Richard Gutwillig, for example, gets suggestions for some of his columns from his editors when they feel an event warrants a piece. "Sometimes," he says, "they're stronger than suggestions." Food writers often benefit from the seasonal schedules. Knowing that in August they'll talk about garden produce, in December, holidays, and in February, Valentine's Day, offers them themes to focus on.

General reading. Newspapers, magazines, journals, newsletters, professional writings, press releases, comic strips—the printed word anywhere—can generate column ideas. Whenever you read an item that piques your interest, let your mind wander. Religion columnist George Plagenz, who likes topical ideas, gets many from looking at newspapers. After reading about the Philadelphia garbage strike of the summer of 1986, for instance, Plagenz composed an inspirational column on "who's going to do the dirty work." Bill Kurtzeborn of the *St. Louis Post-Dispatch* writes a twice-weekly bits-and-pieces feature called "Headhunter," in which he culls headlines from news stories or tidbits from current happenings and pens snappy one-liners about them. Every day, he goes through newspapers with scissors or penknife in hand, stalking potential targets for his wry comments.

Be a prolific picker-upper. You never know when a handout will generate a column idea. At tourist information centers, supermarkets, county and state fairs, grab fistfuls of free literature on local businesses, governments, and organizations. That brochure on a local flood-relief organization may provide an interesting topic for your community service column.

Mailing lists. Writers place their names on mailing lists for organizations, trade groups, universities, travel bureaus, and businesses so they will get press releases, newsletters, fliers, brochures, and product samples. And those pesky "bingo" cards in the back of magazines on which you can check off and send away for all manner of free information about advertised products and services are a writer's dream. In return for one minute of circling, mail flows in for weeks.

For her syndicated "Beauty Briefs" feature, Florence De Santis pores over printed material and tries products routed her way by public relations offices. Grace Hechinger receives releases on new studies and college programs that she writes about in her education column for *Glamour*. Computer columnist Bob Schwabach is on the mailing lists of many computer hardware and software firms, and the literature and products he receives help him keep his idea bank replenished.

Libraries. Libraries are another good source of ideas. Try leafing through magazines you don't ordinarily receive and newspapers from other cities. Journals, dissertation abstracts, government publications, and periodicals in your field or in a related one can keep you in touch with the latest information, studies, ideas, and research.

Phone directories and classified ads. The yellow pages or classified newspaper ads can trigger all kinds of potential topics. "Four-year-old bicycle for sale" could suggest a nostalgia piece on learning to ride a bike or a factual column on how two-wheelers have evolved over the years. Yellow pages listings for cleaning services could spark a consumer column installment on choosing one, on how difficult good help is to find, or on the high price of getting someone to dust and vacuum your home.

Television, movies, radio. Television—not only newscasts but documentaries and even sitcoms—provides writers with column material. Even while driving down the highway with the radio tuned to a deejay, news program, or call-in show, columnists find ideas. *Grand Rapids Press*'s John Douglas, who views movies in his role as film critic, gets material for his social commentary columns from them. "Movies help," he says. "They tend to keep your brain stirred up." The controversial film *The Color Purple*, for example, generated many pieces by social essayists on the portrayal of blacks.

Wire services. Staff newspaper columnists with access to Reuters, Associated Press, and UPI can use wire-service news stories as jumping-off points for columns. Bill Speers, who writes "Newsmakers," a celebrity column in the *Philadelphia Inquirer*, gets ideas and information for each of his bits-and-pieces segments from different wire services as well as from press agents and the many newspapers he reads. At the end of each installment of his column, he credits the print sources he has used.

Recycling. As we've noted before, queries from readers have kindled many a column idea, and they're staples of the Q&A columnist's diet. But when you're just starting and your mailbox hasn't yet filled up, or if you get the same questions over and over again by different readers, you may have to invent some questions.

Other alternatives once your column is underway are to devote an occasional column to an in-depth narrative on an issue making news or on one that recurs in readers' letters. For example, a nutrition Q&A columnist suffering from letter deficiency might devote a whole column to the latest information on minimum daily intake of vitamins and minerals.

If you do decide to repeat a question, don't scrimp and reprint both the old question and old answer. By all means, resurrect an evergreen, but compose a new answer. Readers can amaze you with how much attention they pay to what you've written, and they'll let you hear about it if you duplicate your old reply word for word.

Series. Try to come up with an idea that lends itself to a series, says *In Business* magazine columnist Jerry Feigen. For example, Feigen recently penned a successful three-parter: one column on banking, another on financial services, and the third on public money. This series provided a comprehensive overview of sources of venture capital, and the continuity carried his audience's interest from one month to the next. When a subject is too complex for one column, a series is a natural.

To Consider: What sources can you tap for your column? Do you need a network of sources? If so, whom can you include in it? How can you reach them?

5
Marketing Your Column

There's no such thing as a closet columnist. Columnists require an audience—someone to hear their arguments, ask their opinion, solicit their help, appreciate their reminiscences. To get your audience, you've got to take your literary treasures out of the closet and get them before an editor's eye. In turn, the editor will appraise them and decide if readers will value them.

Starting Small Versus Going for the Big Time

Your work may have to pass under the magnifying glasses of many editors before you make a sale. Since so many columnists already flood pages of newsprint with their words, the competition is keen. The more original your concept, the more finely honed your writing, and the more carefully targeted your market, the greater the chance of seeing your feature in print. But keep in mind that most aspiring columnists have to start small.

Sometimes beginners even offer a short run of their column for free so that an editor can test reader response and writer responsibility. Look at this strategy as an introductory offer much like the free samples of soap, shampoo, and cereal that manufacturers use to entice consumers. If you do decide to work gratis for a paying publication, set a time limit that both you and the editor agree on, and try bartering for at least a subscription or classified ad in return for your services.

Syndicated columnist Vicki Williams got her start this way. For years she'd filled a personal journal with her opinions and reactions to political events, secretly wanting to share her musings with the world. One day she typed her journal entries and sent them to the Wabash *Plain Dealer*. "I knew I should start locally," she remembers, "so I sent in some sample copies, but I never did hear from them." Refusing to let her dream die that easily, she went down to talk to the editor in person. Still no decision. Again, she approached him, this time with a new gambit. "I said I would write the column in return for a subscription to the paper for ninety days if they would print my column [during that time] and see what kind of response they got." It worked. Less than a year later she was syndicated by King Features. Of her stint as an unpaid columnist she says, "I knew this was an investment in myself." An investment that paid off handsomely, we might add.

Remember, when starting small, there may be perks that compensate for low or no pay. Film, theater, and music columnists often receive free tickets. Recreation writers get lessons and new experiences like rope climbing and white-water rafting without taking out their wallets. Invitations to various events—trade shows, receptions, galas, openings—come with the title "columnist." At the very least, you'll gain an opportunity to practice your craft and you'll end up with tear sheets that you can place in your portfolio.

In trying to find a home for your column, what sorts of publications should you consider? And what are your chances of success with them?

Newspapers carry by far the most columns and provide the most likely market for new ones. Beginning columnists should probably stick to publications within 100 miles or so of their work or home (you Alaskans and Texans, with all that space, can think bigger). As John R. Starr, managing editor of the *Arkansas Democrat*, says, "Unless a column comes through a syndicate, which means it's been screened, we're not likely to take it, if it's from out of state." However, he continues, "I do read very closely all the local material submitted."

> *Syndicated humor columnist Art Buchwald's advice for beginning columnists: "Don't come to me for a job. That's the most important thing. . . ."*

> *"Try to start with a newspaper. I'm here because I started off writing for newspapers. You're not paid much but you learn to write to space and you learn discipline."—Dee Hardie,* House Beautiful *columnist.*

Smaller newspapers offer a greater opportunity for a freelancer to break in. The competition isn't as keen and the editors are more likely to take a chance on an unknown. Don't expect a large paycheck here; you might not receive more than five or ten dollars per installment. As a matter of fact, on the littlest publications you may not get any money at all, but the credential will be a block you can build your career with. Writing for one of these papers gives novices a chance to perfect a column before heading for the big time. However, a timely, well-executed idea directed at the right paper, might let you crack one of those larger, more elusive markets on the first try.

Syndicates like King Features, News America, and Tribune

Media Services act as brokers, selling a column to several newspapers at one time. While they accept over-the-transom submissions and offer a potential market for beginners, the competition is fierce. Since you're up against experienced writers and columnists, a unique, timely, and well-executed idea or column that's already in print and has an established audience will garner the most attention in this market. (Turn to Chapter Seven for more information.)

Magazines run longer columns than do newspapers, but they print fewer. Without a track record, a contact at the publication, or celebrity status, it's highly unlikely you'll crack the magazine market right away. However, just as in the newspaper world, smaller publications that can't afford big names will gamble on a newcomer more readily than their larger counterparts. Here again, paychecks depend on the size of the publication, ranging from nothing on tiny alternative publications to 50 to 100 dollars on midsize monthlies to 500 dollars and up at major magazines.

Newsletters are an often overlooked market. These specialized publications abound in all sorts of fields—health food, business, education, parenting, pharmaceuticals, travel, to name a few.

Be aware that some newsletters are single-person operations, and some don't carry columns at all. But beginners, particularly, shouldn't dismiss these publications, because they might be just the place to test an idea and establish credentials.

Some bigger newsletters, like the sixteen-page monthly *The Newsletter of Parenting*, carry several columns. Cathy Johnson, the editorial coordinator, signs her columnists to twelve-month contracts and encourages reader submissions to a monthly parenting column written by and for mothers and fathers of very young children. For a column of 500 to 1,000 words, she pays $100. Smaller newsletters usually deal more informally with contributors and provide less recompense ($25 or less) for the work.

Company or in-house publications, whether newspaper, newsletter, or magazine format, provide a limited market for aspiring columnists. In most cases, you must work for the firm or organization to get a regular slot on the page. But even if you're not an employee, you might approach an editor at a corporation with an offer to freelance a column. The size of the paycheck will depend on what you can negotiate. For guidelines, look at the "How Much Should I Charge" section of *Writer's Market*. Fraternal and professional groups also put out magazines or journals geared toward their membership.

Shoppers, those free nonsubscription newspapers you pick up at shopping malls, stores, restaurants, or other commercial enterprises, are another place to look for column space. Since the idea behind these publications is to promote groups of merchants, any kind of column (service, community, entertainment, etc.) geared to pull in more readers might win you a go-ahead. Again, payment varies, but most shoppers are low-budget publications.

Advertising columns, which plug products, services, or amusements, stand as a special market apart from the mainstream. Here, the writer convinces a market—an advertising agency, advertiser(s), or a group of merchants—to pay for an ongoing column ballyhooing their products or services. Then the agency, advertiser(s), or merchants contract with a publication, paying it to run the column-ad on a regular basis. One writer, Al Counts, approached a local liquor store with a suggestion that he write a continuing column featuring different wines in each installment. The store accepted the proposal and was pleased when this unique ad brought in many more customers than had their standard ad. Another example of this kind of feature is "Korry's Comments" carried by the Toronto *Globe and Mail*. In this regularly scheduled column-ad, Saul Korman touts Canadian couture, hotels, and other establishments in a bits-and-pieces, first-person format.

Newspaper, magazine, newsletter, company publication, shopper—which should you try? Begin by considering the following.

Is your column strictly local, or does it have regional or national appeal? For example, if you're writing a society column, it's probably a local subject. In most cases, readers of *The New*

York Times wouldn't want to hear about parties, marriages, and charity balls in Lexington, Kentucky, unless the principals were jet-setters who frequented the New York scene.

Who is your audience? Suppose you want to do a computer column. Do you want to reach entrepreneurs, computer programmers, or owners of personal computers? Your style, your focus, the degree of complexity of the subject matter, and the markets you approach will depend on whom you want to read the column. For example, newspaper life-style sections are a potential market for a general computer column while business publications and business sections of newspapers are possibilities for features geared toward commercial applications.

How often do you hope to see your column appearing? Does the subject lend itself to daily, weekly, or monthly publication? If you envision your personal advice column as a daily feature, it makes no sense to approach a monthly publication. Likewise, if you're planning a once-a-month column on coping with stress, a daily paper probably won't go for it.

What is the goal of your column? To entertain, inform, inspire, motivate, bring in customers, generate publicity? A combination of these? If attracting customers or producing publicity is your goal, you'd better combine it with a more altruistic or reader-oriented purpose. With the exception of shoppers, few publications take on blatantly self-serving columns.

Again, many times what you want to accomplish will influence where you try to publish. If you direct a mental health center and would like to educate the public on mental health issues while generating clients, a column in a local paper discussing modern maladies makes sense. If your goal is to educate as many people as you can, then going to a larger or national publication will accomplish your purpose more effectively.

Finding Your Best Markets

Now think about what kinds of publications your audience would most likely read. Consider both general- and specific-audience periodicals. As you evaluate various possible markets, see if you can come up with an original combination of subject and audience. Finding an untapped audience will increase the probability of getting a byline. Suppose you want to reach the owners of personal computers. Have you considered making your focus even more specialized? How about a women's business magazine or a parents' newsletter?

To find the names of different publications look at the following.

• *Gale Directory of Publications* (formerly *The IMS/Ayer Directory of Publications*). Located in the reference section of libraries, the *Gale Directory* lists daily and weekly newspapers, shoppers, and newsletters by geographic area, with addresses and telephone numbers for each. It also lists newsletters by subject.

• *Writer's Market*. This annual directory lists magazine markets and a few newspaper sections and newsletters. Each entry details audience, needs, and submission hints. However, not all listings carry information specifically on columns.

• *Newsletters Directory*. This directory contains addresses and telephone numbers of newsletters, plus editors' names and information about the publications, such as purpose, content, and frequency. Entries are indexed by subject, publisher, and title.

• *The Standard Periodical Directory*. This directory lists more than 60,000 newsletters, magazines, and newspapers in the US and Canada. Newspapers are listed geographically. Magazines and newsletters are listed by subject. Entries include addresses and phone numbers of publications, as well as editors' names.

As you would do with any sort of freelance writing, write for sample copies and writer's guidelines of possible magazine and newsletter markets, pick up copies of different periodicals on the newsstand, or browse through them at the library. Also, ask friends to be on the lookout for potential homes for your column, and don't forget to peruse publications as you wait for appointments with the dentist, doctor, or lawyer. Their offices are often a source of magazines that are strangers to you.

> *"My pet peeve is people who don't take the time to study the newsletter or those who send out reams of photocopied submissions to every name in the publishing directory."*— *Cathy Johnson, editorial coordinator for* The Newsletter of Parenting.

Read each potential market from cover to cover. Don't skip the letters to the editors, the ads, the editor's column, or editorial page. They'll give you a mini-demographic report on a publication's readers—their interests, likes, dislikes, income level, biases. As you examine each publication, consider the following:

• Does the publication already carry a regular feature on your subject? If so, they're probably not a market for you, but don't put the publication aside yet. See what your competitor does. How does your column differ? Can you pick up any tips or ideas from the competition?

• If the publication doesn't carry a column like yours, would yours complement or enhance the publication? How?

• Would your column appeal to the publication's readers? Why?

• What about the other columns in the publication? Is there a consistent style? Will yours blend in?

• What about the publication's philosophy? Again, will your column fit in? If you're a die-hard conservative and the magazine espouses the liberal viewpoint, it probably wouldn't be interested in what you have to say.

• Who are the advertisers? Will your column clash with them? For example, a muckraking feature on pharmaceuticals probably wouldn't sell to a magazine kept afloat by revenue from drug company ads.

To Do: Make a list of possible markets for your feature. After you're done, tack up the list and add to it over the next few days. During this time, continue to link your subject to different audiences. Does this bring any other markets to mind?

To Do: Take out a sheet of paper and divide it into five sections with these headings: publication, audience, slant, advantages, and disadvantages. Under publication, write down the names of possible markets from the list you made earlier. Then set aside a block of time to fill in the other four sections. For each publication, jot down the audience and what column slant would work best. (Although you chose a slant in Chapter Two, you may decide to modify it based on the publications you've chosen to target.) In the last two rows, list all the advantages and disadvantages of writing for each publication (that is, low pay, good exposure, contacts you'd make, perfect fit with audience). For an example, see page 76.

Your list can be any length, depending on your subject matter and the number of suitable periodicals. Remember to include even publications you feel are iffy markets. The weeding out process won't begin until all your possibilities are down in black and white.

To Consider: The next step is to determine which of these publications you really want to approach and in what order. Sometimes just completing the chart will clarify the decision. Other times, the choice will be difficult. Systems of decision making have been designed to turn making up your mind into a science, but frankly, it boils down to a question of which market fits your goals, needs, expectations, and subject matter. When you're done with your list, try to come up with an order of preference for your markets.

Your Submission Packet

Before contacting an editor, you'll need to put together a packet containing a proposal, six to eight sample columns, support-

SAMPLE WORKSHEET FOR A COMPUTER COLUMN

PUBLICATION	AUDIENCE	SLANT	ADVANTAGES	DISADVANTAGES
Timbuktu Times	General small-town	General information on computers, software, applications	1. No computer column yet 2. Probably not too difficult to break into 3. Possibility of weekly column	1. Not affluent audience 2. Little or no pay 3. Small circulation
Gulch City Gazette	General small-city	General information on computers, software, applications	1. No computer column yet 2. Probably not too difficult to break into 3. Varied and affluent audience 4. Dynamic, progressive paper 5. Possibility of weekly column	1. Little pay 2. Small circulation but larger than Times
Working Parents	Parents of young children	Helping your child learn games	1. No computer column yet 2. Big circulation 3. Audience values education 4. Excellent credential	1. A lot of competition 2. May want writer with strong credentials 3. Column would have to be monthly

ing material (as appropriate), and a self-addressed, stamped envelope.

Your packet should be neatly typed, businesslike, error-free, and professional-looking. Misspellings and sloppy typing flag a writer as careless and undependable.

Use pica or elite type (no script) on $8\frac{1}{2}'' \times 11''$ white bond paper. No erasable paper or onion skin, and no strange colors, please. The excitement should be in the words, not in fancy trappings. Use ample margins (at least $1\frac{1}{4}$ inches at top, bottom, and sides). And always use a dark, black ribbon so the text is easy to read. Those with dot-matrix printers should enhance the print if the machine has that capability.

THE PROPOSAL The proposal is your sales pitch, and it can be presented as either one long (one- to two-page) letter or a one- to two-page promotion piece with a separate, short cover letter. Regardless of the form you choose, the proposal should include the following information:

- Subject and slant of your column.
- Title, if it's catchy or particularly apropos.
- Your credentials—writing, as well as any that pertain to the subject matter you're covering.
- Statement of audience appeal—telling why readers would be interested in your column, pointing out any gaps in editorial matter your column might fill and how your offering would increase readership.
- Statement of your intention to follow up with a phone call to discuss your proposal, indicating a specific week about fourteen days hence as the time you'll get back to the editor.
- Additional ideas for installments other than those in your sample columns, to let your editor know this isn't a one-shot series and that you can generate topics easily.

The letter proposal presents all of this vital information in straight narrative (see page 79 for an example), while the promotion piece proposal is more flexible in format. For instance, you might set your page up with simple headings like *column idea*, *audience*, and *credentials* and include the relevant information under each category. Or you might substitute clever headings if your subject lends itself to that style and you think the publication will be receptive. For example:

What's cooking? (Here is where Dinah introduces her new column, including the title [if she's got one], kind of format, topics she'll cover, and frequency of the column.)

Who's in the kitchen? (Dinah gives her credentials here.)

Guess who's coming to dinner? (Dinah tells why the publication's readership would be interested in this column.)

Because there is no set format for the promotion piece, you can be creative, but make sure it is easy to read. You can type the proposal, do it on your word processor, or have it professionally designed and printed. But remember that window dressing will not win the job for you. Idea, content, and style will.

Whether you choose the letter proposal or the promotion piece with cover letter, set up the letter in standard business letter format. If you have your own business stationery, in white or a light neutral color, use it. If your telephone number is not on the letterhead or if you're not using printed stationery, be sure to include the phone number with the area code.

Always address the letter to an individual, not "Dear Editor." A quick phone call or a look at a recent masthead should give you the appropriate editor's name. When there's any doubt as to gender, as in names like Pat and Chris, initial names like M. K. Smith, or foreign or unusual names like Vishnu, check it out.

Remember, neither the letter proposal nor the promotion piece should run more than one to two pages. After all, editors are busy, and they expect columnists to write succinctly. And keep the tone businesslike—this is no time to be folksy, and you won't earn points for gushing about either the publication or your column. Prove your worth with your samples.

PREPARING SAMPLE COLUMNS Because samples are so important in convincing an editor to take you on as a columnist, you'll want to make sure they're impressive individually and as

DINAH DEMPSEY

3121 Redmond Drive   406-555-1212
La Plata, Montana 50000

Edie Prestwood, Food Editor   July 28, 19—
La Plata Daily
31 Linden Way
La Plata, Montana 50000

Dear Ms. Prestwood:

Cooking for one needn't be an exercise in frustration. No longer will a bachelor living alone have to choke down lasagna for twelve days straight because he couldn't figure out how to cut the recipe. Neither will the single woman, having divided her ingredients precisely by two, have to spoon soup instead of souffle because half of each ingredient didn't equal half a souffle. Never again will the widow be left with a refrigerator of partially used containers of tomato paste, sour cream, garbanzo beans, buttermilk, and coconut after she's used dribs and drabs in her culinary creations.

My proposed column, "One in the Kitchen with Dinah," will feature cooking for the solo eater. I'll offer recipes created and tested by me to feed the person who eats alone. This column, which I envision running once a week, will include coordinated menus to use up those leftover ingredients one never knows what to do with. This feature will also include tips for cutting down existing recipes and making them work. Occasionally, a column will be devoted to readers' questions and tips that they've sent in.

As the recent Greater La Plata Survey shows, there has been an upswing in single-person households among both young unmarrieds and senior citizens in the area. But the appeal of my column is even wider. Couples with conflicting schedules will find this feature helpful for nights when one of them is dining home alone. Families where one member won't or can't have what the others eat also will find my column useful.

Since no other paper in the region carries this kind of feature, I feel that my column will draw an audience, not just of readers who ordinarily devour the food pages but of those who have been skipping them because recipes have been geared toward feeding four or more.

I was an instructor at the Bon Vivant Cooking Academy in San Francisco for five years and authored a booklet of recipes for the Academy.

Enclosed are eight sample columns and a copy of my recipe booklet. I also am including a self-addressed stamped envelope. I will call you the week of August 15th to discuss my proposal.

Thank you for your consideration.

Very truly yours,

Dinah Dempsey

a group. After completing them, go back and revise, then revise again. Put them away for several days, then read them as a package. Do they give a representative picture of the kind of column you want to write? Are they your best work? Would you buy them? Try them on a friend or colleague who will be honest and objective—another writer, a journalism instructor, an expert in your subject matter. Weigh all criticisms and suggestions, then make those changes you feel were well advised.

Type your sample columns, using standard, double-spaced manuscript format. If you're using a computer, turn off the right justification.

The opening page of each column should begin approximately one third of the way down the paper, with the headline for the installment centered about 3/4″ (that's two double spaces) above the beginning of the text. The ongoing name of your column, if you have one, should be placed in capital letters at the upper left-hand corner, and your name, address, and telephone number should be typed in the upper right-hand corner of the first page.

On subsequent pages, place your last name and a header (an identifying tag, taking a word from the title and one from the headline) in the upper left-hand corner. For example, our Dinah Dempsey might use "Dempsey/KITCHEN/Lasagna." Number succeeding pages of each installment in the upper right-hand corner. Indicate the end of each column with the newspaper symbol 30, ##, or The End, centered one double-spaced line below the last line of text. (See examples, page 82.)

Paper clip each column separately. Do not staple.

COMPLETING THE PACKET You may want to include additional material, such as clips, to strengthen your case for becoming a columnist. Dinah's letter proposal, for instance, mentions that she's enclosing her recipe booklet. Don't inundate the editor with supporting material, however. Include only a few clips, and choose only those that are relevant to the subject matter of your column or that show your writing style to advantage.

Include a self-addressed, stamped envelope. If you don't want your samples returned in the event they're rejected, enclose a letter-size SASE for the editor's reply and note in your cover letter that the manuscripts need not be mailed back. If you do want your samples returned, enclose an SASE large enough to hold the manuscripts and with sufficient postage. If you plan to send the same samples out again, paperclip a piece of cardboard to the packet to prevent folding, and stamp or write "Do Not Bend" on the envelope.

Dempsey/KITCHEN/Lasagna   2

great accompaniment for any lasagna is a crisp green salad and garlic bread, always.............................

ONE IN THE KITCHEN WITH DINAH

Dinah Dempsey
3121 Redmond Drive
La Plata, MN 50000
406-555-1212

Lasagna for One

Is your relationship with lasagna a love/hate affair? You adore the taste of this nutritious dish for one day, or two, or maybe three, but by the beginning of the second week you never want to see a forkful of pasta again.

Approaching the Editor

In most cases, the best method is to approach one publication at a time, waiting until that editor makes a decision before going on to the next. Editors like to feel they're getting an exclusive look and that the column has been tailored to their readership. They may resent being one hit in a scattershot approach.

However, if you have a topic that is time-limited, particularly one that is riding the crest of a media wave, then sending the same proposal to several markets at the same time might be justified. In this case, be sure to point out that you've sent the submission out to several publications simultaneously because of the immediacy of the subject. (Don't, however, fool yourself into thinking your idea fits into this hurry-up category if, in fact, it doesn't, or you'll just end up annoying the people you want to impress.)

> *"You've got to be a salesman. Your product is information. You have to tell the editors what you can do for them and how you can increase circulation by interesting the community in what you write."*—George Hamersley. Mainland Journal *feature writer and former columnist for* The *(Ocean City-Somers Point, N.J.)* Record.

There are two ways to initiate your approach to the editor: by phone or by mail.

Editors generally prefer receiving column queries by mail because it allows them to review a proposal at a time that's convenient for them. It also lets them give some thought to an idea before talking to its creator. With a phone call an unknown runs the risk of catching an editor at an inopportune moment, when he or she can't give a proposal thorough consideration.

However, many successful columnists have pitched their initial proposals over the phone. If you're confident about picking up the receiver and hitting an editor with a sales spiel cold, it's worth a try. Do some homework before lifting the phone. Be prepared to give a brief description of your column and why it should interest the publication's readership—in essence, you'll need to convey the same information you'd include in a written proposal, but do it quickly. Practice your oral version first on your spouse, your kids, your dog. When you're happy with it, call the publication. Make sure you ask to be connected with the appropriate editor and that you have the correct spelling and pronunciation of his or her name (if you're uncertain, ask the receptionist). Once you've reached the editor, introduce yourself and give your sales pitch.

Don't expect a decision on the spot. A phone query rarely substitutes for sending written material. Instead, think of it primarily as a chance to get your foot in the door—an opportunity to make personal contact and pique the editor's interest in reviewing your material.

If the editor is reluctant to discuss your idea in detail, don't stay on the phone too long and risk losing a sale. And even if the editor does sound interested, close your presentation with an offer to send samples, and do so. It's a good idea to send your entire packet, and you might want to remind the editor of your phone conversation in your letter.

The amount of time an editor takes to review a proposal and sample manuscripts varies from publication to publication. Some reply within a week or so, while others hold the proposal for months. A writer is always justified in checking up on a submission after six to eight weeks with either a short note or quick phone call.

The Follow Up

If, in the cover letter, you said you'd be calling, follow through on time, unless the editor has already replied. A follow-up call should be short. Identify yourself, mention your proposal, and before launching into your talk, ask, "Is this a convenient time for you?" If so, begin your pitch or make an appointment to talk in person.

Whether the follow-up conversation takes place by phone or at the editor's office, be prepared to discuss in greater detail the points you've already made in the cover letter: overall column idea, possible topics, the audience, and your credentials. The editor, too, may have suggestions for changes in format or for other topics to cover. Keep an open mind, but not so open that you, the hard rock aficionado, end up reviewing classical music records—unless you really do feel that flexible and/or you think that doing one job will eventually lead to the other.

Even though it's a buyers' market, keep in mind that you're interviewing the editor as much as the editor is interviewing you. Do you really want to work for and with that person? Does the editor want to alter the concept beyond what you want it to be? You won't be in a position to be very picky at this stage, but remember this is someone you're going to have to work with.

The editor may accept or reject the column on the spot, or ask for time to think about it. In that case, it's perfectly acceptable to ask when the editor expects to get back to you, and ask if you can phone if you don't receive a reply by that date.

No matter what the outcome, send the editor a thank-you note to show appreciation for the time and consideration given your work and to be remembered kindly. It's not unheard-of for an editor to change his or her mind or for the publication to take a new direction—one in which your column might fit after all. Five minutes' worth of effort in writing a note may reap unexpected dividends.

What to do When the Editor Accepts

After you're done jumping up and down for joy, you need to have a serious chat with your new boss. Before the final handshake, however, consider the following questions and points and use them as a guide for negotiating with the editor:

- How often will the column appear? How much lead time will the editor want? Can you submit the columns one at a time or should you submit them in bunches?
- How will you be paid and how much? Will you receive a set fee per column, an hourly rate, or be paid by the column inch? Will you be a freelancer or on staff? Will the publication pay on receipt of each column or at regular intervals? Will the publication expect you to submit a bill?
- What rights will the publication be buying? (See the appendix for an explanation of copyright.)
- Will you be able to review the editing? (Probably not on a newspaper, which carries a short deadline.)

Negotiating for money is difficult for most writers (and for people in most walks of life). There is more than one way to determine a reasonable fee: ask the editor what the publication typically pays, or find out what other columnists on that publication make. (Remember that freelancers should compare their fees to the fees of other freelancers, staff writers to those of other staffers.)

If the editor does not send you a written contract, mail him or her a letter of confirmation stating the details. Include the title or subject of your column, its frequency, your deadline schedule, etc. A letter will help avoid misunderstandings initially and in the future, and it gives both you and the editor the opportunity to straighten out any problems at the start.

Photographs and Illustrations

Some columns requre illustrations or photographs to display a product, clarify a concept, or show how to fix or construct an item. When working out contractual arrangements with an editor, you should also discuss how any photos or illustrations for your column will be handled. In some cases, the writer provides finished drawings or photographs, done personally or by others. Or an editor may assign a staff photographer or illustrator to do the work (the illustrator may be aided by a rough sketch the writer has submitted). In other cases, the publication or syndicate may contract with a freelance artist or photographer for pictures.

Interior design columnist Rita St. Clair uses photographs supplied by designers, manufacturers, and public relations people to illustrate the decorating principles and ideas she discusses in her columns.

Colonial Homes's Dorothy Hammond, on the other hand, relies on reader-submitted shots in her Q&A antiques column. Along with queries about items like buttocks baskets, wooden noggins, hooked rugs, and Chippendale chairs, her correspondents provide photographs of the item in question to help Hammond identify and value it. If the quality of the picture is good enough to reproduce, she includes it in the column along with her answer.

As for a photograph of the writer, that's an editorial decision made by each publication. A columnist may be allowed to choose which shot will be used (in democratic fashion, Roger Simon once ran five photos of himself in his column and let readers vote for their favorite), but usually the decision rests higher up. In fact, some syndicated columnists, like Ellen Goodman, have their faces looking out at us in some papers but not others.

Dealing with Rejection

Expect rejection. Your column idea will be "not right for us," "not right for us at this time," "just like something we already have," "just like something that failed here fifteen years ago." Don't take these turndowns personally. Try other publications. However, if you get a number of rejections (that number depends on your subject and the size of your market), reevaluate your column and market choices.

Whenever you get an encouraging rejection, whether a handwritten line on a form letter, a personal note, or a turn-down over the phone or in person, ask the editor for any ideas about other markets or any suggestions to improve the column. When you ask people for advice, most are willing to help if they can. With luck, you may even make some contacts that will help you place your column.

No matter what, be persistent. More than a few good column ideas sit at the bottom of writers' desk drawers because their creators have been discouraged by rejections. And more than a few would-be columnists have seen their rejected and shelved idea pop up in a different paper where another, more determined competitor persevered to find the right home for the feature.

Persistence also pays off for staff reporters wanting to rise to the hallowed halls of columndom. Staffers should fan their dreams of being a columnist by periodically reminding their editors of their goal.

Mike Levine knew he wanted to be a columnist since his high school days in New York City, when he would devour the words of Jimmy Breslin, Jimmy Cannon, and Pete Hamill as he rode to school on the subway. A few years later, while working as a reporter at the *Times Herald-Record* in Middletown, New York, he saw his chance. "For three years I kept telling the editor 'I want a column.' In 1983 the editor put his neck on the line and I got my column." Today residents of the Catskill Mountain area read Levine's commentary three times a week.

Other Approaches to Breaking In

While most columnists enter the profession in traditional ways (moving up from staff writer to columnist or marketing a saleable idea over the transom), others come in by a variety of side doors. Here are some other ways columnists have gotten their start. Perhaps their stories will alert you to some alternate roads to a column-writing career.

Write a guest column and be discovered. Freelance a few opinion columns to the op-ed section of your newspaper. If you write well, on interesting subjects, you may be asked to come on as a regular. Or once you've established a track record with the paper, you may find your proposal for a continuing column is given more serious consideration.

For years, Paul Deegan lived in Connecticut and worked as a defense industry executive. But about every two months, he'd put together a social commentary piece for the op-ed page of the Bridgeport *Post*. Then in 1985, he retired from his nine-to-five job and moved to Florida. No sooner had the rays from the subtropical sun warmed him than he put pen to paper and dashed off a piece chronicling his trek down from New England. He posted it, along with a clipping or two from the Bridgeport paper, to the *Boca Raton News*. Three days later he got an offer to write a regular column. He agreed and went on to become a member of the editorial board of the *News* as well.

Write a letter to the editor. One day, in a puckish mood, *Grand Rapids Press* film reviewer John Douglas got the urge to comment on several local issues, so he wrote and mailed a couple of tongue-in-cheek letters to his editor. The letters, meant only for Douglas's and his editor's private entertainment, were not intended for print, but the editor enjoyed them so much he asked Douglas to do a twice-weekly local commentary. Today Douglas's column has expanded to four times a week.

Know the right someone. The trick here is not only knowing someone who can put your column into print but having authority or expertise of your own in a particular field. Cheryl Lee Terry was enjoying a successful business as a numerologist and hand reader when one day, unbeknownst to her, a client of hers who worked for *Elle* told one of the magazine's editors, "You've just got to get Cheryl Lee Terry to write a numerology column." *Elle* made an offer. "I promptly turned them down," Terry remembers, "I didn't think it was a good idea." Eventually she relented, and, judging from the stacks of fan mail she gets, *Elle* readers are thrilled she did.

Write a good book. Sometimes a nonfiction book can be parlayed into an ongoing feature and get you noticed. Experts with publication history and high visibility have an inside track in garnering a regular feature. *Savvy* magazine approached Betty Lehan Harragan on the basis of her best-selling book *Games Mother Never Taught You*. "They knew me through my book and personally," Harragan recalls. "What do you think women want?" the editors asked her as she stepped into her role as columnist. She showed them. For two and a half years Harragan fielded questions about business concerns from her readers. Then in 1982, her column took up residence in *Working Woman*, where it still draws mailbags full of letters.

Be in the right place at the right time. This isn't something one can always plan, but to a large degree you make your own luck by going where writers congregate or where people in your field gather.

While attending a Sigma Delta Chi journalism fraternity dinner at American University, syndicated columnist Jack Anderson told a professor that he was looking for young talent. The professor told Joseph Spear, who was hosting the dinner, about the opening. Since Spear's goal was to be a feature writer, not an investigative reporter, he didn't jump at the opportunity. But after he mulled the idea over, he decided to give it a try. Published clips in hand, Spear trooped down to Anderson's office where, after composing some sample columns, he got the job.

"I'm living testimony," says Spear, now an editor with the Anderson organization, "to a belief and theory of mine, that it is not enough to be talented and ambitious—God knows, there are a ton of ambitious and talented people out there— but you have to be in the right place at the right time."

Be in the right place at the wrong time. Former *Cleveland Press* religion editor George Plagenz walked into his managing editor's office late one Friday afternoon back in 1978 and pitched the idea of a rate-the-churches religion column. The editor nodded yes and Plagenz happily went off to pen his feature. Simple, wasn't it? It was only later, after his column had settled into its niche, that Plagenz found out that the editor had not thought much of the idea that Friday afternoon. He had given Plagenz a go-ahead only because it was the end of the week and he was in a rush to get home. "Yes" didn't require any more of his time but "no" would have.

6
Promoting Your Column

Whether your column is the Rolls-Royce of writing or a good solid Honda, a little bit of publicity can get your words to more people and into more papers. While nothing beats word-of-mouth acclaim for ensuring your column a permanent spot in a publication, a well-thought-out publicity campaign will add fans to your roster.

If you're syndicated, you should have some sort of agreement with the syndicate (ideally spelled out in your contract) about what promotion it will do for your column. Since the name of the game in syndication is the number of papers that buy a column, it is advantageous to both you and the syndicate to have information about you and your column before the public frequently. However, the amount and kind of publicity will vary from agency to agency.

Some syndicates, like United Feature and its sister company

NEA (Newspaper Enterprise Association), in addition to advertising their writers, work to get stories about them placed in trade magazines. If a columnist wants, the two syndicates will also arrange for appearances on television and radio talk shows. On the other hand, smaller outfits like The Washington Post Writers Group focus on marketing columns to newspapers, leaving additional promotion up to the writer.

Newspapers and magazines, too, tout the columnists who liven their pages, with anything from in-publication one-inch teasers to full-page ads. Or they'll sing the praises of a writer in a television or radio spot for their periodical. Columnists have even taken the journey to fame with their name plastered on the side of a bus or hung from a streamer on the back of an airplane as a newspaper heralds them as one of the benefits of buying the publication.

In other instances, most or all of the publicity is up to the writer. Small-town and self-syndicated columnists usually end up doing their own touting and shouting, seeking out speaking engagements, radio and television shows, and other opportunities to get name and column before the public. Self-syndicated writers, and those who would like to be, will find that self-promotion and the ensuing recognition make a feature more attractive to additional editors, which may mean more sales.

Start thinking now about how you'll promote your column. If you come up with a clever idea, you can incorporate it into your marketing package. Read through the following suggestions and use any you feel will help publicize your column. Work out a promotion campaign, scheduling activities into your calendar at planned intervals.

Buy business cards and stationery imprinted with your name, address, and telephone number, if you haven't already done so. The stationery should be either white or a neutral color. If you want to put life onto the page, do it with colored ink in your letterhead. You can be more creative with your business cards, depending on the impression you want to make and the kind of column you write. Hand out cards whenever you meet an editor, another writer, a resource person, or anyone else you want to remember you.

Get listed. Join writers' organizations and get your name placed in writers' directories. An editor could stumble across your name this way and want to see your column. And as an added benefit, you'll receive invitations to press trips and get more interesting junk mail.

Join organizations in your field and get to know members. Stephen Atlas's membership in several singles groups, including Parents Without Partners, spurred the idea for his first book and his column on single parenting. Now he speaks before these groups all over the country and facilitates seminars for them. Parents Without Partners sponsored his second book, and loyal fans from these chapters read his column and offer information, inspiration, and ideas.

Seek out a variety of groups that would be interested in hearing you speak on your column subject. Look for organizations in different fields. For example, self-syndicated gardening writers Doc and Katy Abraham give talks on plants and on the environment to gardening clubs, Kiwanis and other service organizations, school groups, and home shows. Along with delivering their pro-environment message, the Abrahams get good exposure for their columns.

To approach an organization, don your publicist suit and call one of the officers or the public relations director. Explain who you are and that you're available to talk to groups. At first, you may have to offer to speak for free or for a small honorarium. If an organization says yes, send your promo kit (see the following section). But even if a group can't schedule you as a lecturer now, you may want to send your information anyway, hoping to interest them in having you come at a later date.

You can also hook up with speakers' bureaus at different organizations. For example, an advice columnist could be listed on a community mental health center's roster. A food columnist could investigate national food-related organizations to see if they maintain lists of lecturers. A medical columnist could contact a hospital and join its speakers' group.

Get on television or radio talk shows. Again, the more who see a columnist's face and hear the columnist's voice, the greater his or her following. Many Marylanders who might not have ever read a fishing column know of *The* (Baltimore) *Sun*'s Bill Burton from his television news segments. Who wouldn't be curious about the bearded fellow in the fishing cap, pipe in hand, reporting on fish runs in Chesapeake Bay, ocean tides, and sightings of Canada geese winging across the autumn sky? Many viewers, captivated by his television personality, have turned to his newspaper column.

If you're interested in pursuing electronic media appearances, call stations that carry local talk shows and find out who is in charge of recruiting talent to appear on the show. Once you've found out that person's name, call and explain who you are and that you'd like to be a guest on the show. Be prepared to give a good reason why the audience would like to hear from you, perhaps by tying your expertise into a news or seasonal event. After your discussion, mail a promo kit. Once you've made a name for yourself, producers may start seeking you out. And eventually, you might negotiate a permanent slot in their news programming schedule or become a talk show regular.

Do public service announcements. Offering to appear on television or radio public service spots for nonprofit organizations or charities is not only altruistic but image-enhancing. And if you're promoting a favorite cause, you'll feel especially good about what you're doing.

Get involved in community events. Many times organizers will find you, but if you want publicity, seek them out. Offer to officiate at crab races, judge parades, and taste the apple pies at county fair cooking contests. Be a guest auctioneer at fundraisers or agree to be auctioned off yourself as a dinner companion for a charity-celebrity fundraiser. The ensuing hoopla will increase your visibility. And be sure to announce your participation in your column, if possible.

Over the years New Jersey columnist George Hamersley has been asked to adjudicate everything from beauty competitions to Christmas decoration contests. As a result, the writer is well known in his community. However, there are pitfalls in this kind of activity, he warns, since every competition has not only its winner but its losers. "Don't get involved where someone's vanity is at stake," he cautions. "Some people take these things very seriously. God help you if you don't like their seven-year-old son's finger painting."

Invite queries. Encourage readers to send in questions, even if yours is not a Q&A feature. Or offer booklets and bulletins to readers who write in. For example, some columnists, like syndicated writer Joe Graedon and self-syndicated gardeners Doc and Katy Abraham, give out informative printed materials for little or no charge. One of the yardsticks of a column's success is the mail it draws, and these tactics help generate letters. As a bonus, the Abrahams point out, prepared leaflets provide a way to answer repeated questions without typing up long personal replies.

Stage a publicity stunt. Tie it in with your column, but don't make it too ludicrous. If you're a humor columnist, how about persuading your local government to proclaim "Pun Day in Petersburg" or "Smile in Sullivan County Day"? A book columnist could distribute bookmarks printed with his or her name, the name of the column, and an inspirational message like "Some of my best friends are books."

Send out pre-event press releases to local newspapers and radio and television stations. Whenever you address a group, perform a newsworthy community service, or stage a publicity stunt, mail out a short release detailing the time, place, name of group, your name, subject of the speech, and your credentials. Keep the notice to one or two double-spaced pages. And don't forget to mention the event in your column, if appropriate.

For electronic media, send press releases to the public service director, to the news director, or to the host or producer of a show that might have reason to announce your upcoming talk. For newspapers, mail it to the editor. With bigger publications, address it to the editor of the section you'd like to see your release appear in. How do you know who the editor is? Pick up the phone and find out.

Before sending out a release, do check with the group you're addressing to see if they're doing any promotion. Perhaps they'll take the job of publicizing right out of your hands. But even if they're not doing any, it's common courtesy to let them know what promotion you're doing.

Putting Together
a Promotion Kit

In many of the above cases, you'll want to send out a promotion kit after making an initial contact. If a group you're speaking to wants information on you, if you want to interest a talk show in having you as a guest, or if you want a magazine or newspaper to do a feature on you, send a promo kit. Likewise, if an editor has just bought your column, send one.

What goes into your promo kit is up to you. Any number of items can make up the package. Just keep the pieces relevant, bearing in mind that the purpose of the kit is to sell writer and column. A bio—a short biography or a personal fact sheet—is the only must. Other possible inclusions are columns you've written, articles by or about you, a photograph, and press releases.

The bio. A bio is a one- to two-page capsule of facts about your life and professional accomplishments. Be sure to emphasize your experience, both professional and avocational, in your field and highlight experiences pertinent to your column. For instance, if you're promoting your feature on do-it-yourself home repair, mention the three houses you've renovated, the hexagonal house you've designed and built, or the home repair courses you teach at the community college. Also, state your writing credits, including your column and any other projects you're working on or have completed.

Add interesting personal facts to help you stand out from the crowd. Maybe you live out West in a cave and thump out your writings on an old Remington. Perhaps that black belt you have in karate or the greenhouse where you cultivate prize-winning orchids are totally unimportant to your job as a career advice columnist, but they do show you're a many-faceted person. Many of us find business writer and tycoon Malcolm Forbes more appealing because we know about his hot air ballooning adventures and his fondness for collecting toy soldiers.

Interesting facts make you come alive to the editor, to the garden club, to the radio producer, and make you someone they would like to learn more about. Listing height, weight, age, hair color, or marital status in your bio is not necessary unless these facts pertain to your column or unless you have a particular reason for including them. For example, if you're writing a seniors column, the fact that you're sixty-five is a plus. If you're penning a diet column, mentioning that you used to tip the scales at 300 pounds and for the last four years have weighed a trim 120 indicates you'd have a special rapport with readers.

There is more than one way to set up a bio. You can choose to do it in a list format, resume-style, using no pronouns. Organize it with short headings like *writing experience*, *related experience*, *publications*, *affiliations*, *media experience*, and *awards*, and include a personal section (this is the place where you might put one or two of those informative, and sometimes offbeat, facts about yourself). Pick and choose headings that reflect your background.

Lay out the bio with plenty of white space—that means wide margins and even skipping a line or two between sections. In her bio, syndicated food columnist Barbara Gibbons lists her accomplishments and related facts under eight categories: *newspaper and magazine affiliations*, *books*, *works in progress*, *pamphlets and brochures*, *radio*, *TV*, *media*, *lectures and speaking engagements*, *prior background*, and *professional organizations*.

Another way to do a bio is to set it up like an advertising promotion. Start with a hook, as these examples do:

> *What is life like when you've got 18 kids, a Victorian house begging for repairs, four dogs, three cats, and six*

electronic guitars? Find out how one Minnesotan copes with life in the hectic zone as widower Elvin Houghton chronicles his zany times as father tries to show he knows best.

If you can't stem the tears from your willow's terminal weeping, if all the lifeblood's gone out of your bleeding heart, and your mighty oak is faltering, let Gordon Gaynor give you the cure with some lively advice about the care and feeding of plants and garden.

"Hard-hitting!" proclaims political pundit Betsey Browne.
"Strong opinion backed by solid facts," exclaims noted political observer Will Horowitz.
Whether it's taking on the Russians, lambasting Pentagon overspending, or putting industrial polluters in their place, Reuben Roister tells it as he sees it.

Use your creativity; play around with format and layout. For example, if your column is question-and-answer, why not try writing your bio this way? Even if you're not a Q&A columnist, this format may serve as an excellent promotion tool. (For an idea of how this can work, see Dinah Dempsey's promotion-style idea for a marketing letter in Chapter Five.) Or try a help wanted ad layout, television script design, or whatever. No matter what format you come up with, it should not only allow for individuality but also come across as professional, and it should convey information quickly, succinctly, and clearly. So you know your creativity hasn't gone awry, test market your bio. Give it to another writer, an editor-friend, or a business acquaintance to critique. Show it to people who are going to be honest with you.

In addition to your bio, consider including the following in your promotion kit:

Articles about you. If articles about you have appeared, include photocopies of one or two of the better ones in your package. Barbara Gibbons inserts a copy of a newspaper piece about her that includes the story of how she launched her career. Don't, however, stick in clips of short printed press releases or notices about your speaking to the Rotary. What you want here are articles that give insight into you as a person.

Writings by you. Include three columns and perhaps an article you've authored. Needless to say, choose your best and make your sample representative of your writing.

Photographs. Photographs should be black and white glossies, preferably 8″ by 10″. No slides or color prints. Photos make a presentation more personal—your smiling face could be just the impetus to entice a local reporter to interview you. But photographs are expensive, so send them only to carefully selected targets.

Press releases. Include press releases of prior engagements only if they go beyond the usual who, what, where, and when, and only if they supplement the material already in your portfolio. If you're an advice columnist who has spoken to the American Psychological Association's annual national meeting, include that press release if it contains detailed descriptions of you and what you've done.

Don't overload the packet; tease the recipient into wanting to know more. All the material in your promo kit should be placed loose in a two-pocketed cardboard folder or similar holder. Address it to the individual in the organization who is in the position to help you. Then mail the packet, along with a short covering letter, first class.

7
Syndicating and Self-Syndicating

Sooner or later many columnists get the itch to be read by millions. The cure they seek for this restless desire is called syndication, having a column appear in several newspapers at the same time. The way they take the cure is either to self-syndicate the column—marketing it themselves to a string of newspapers—or to approach an established syndicate to broker their column for them.

Syndication, whether on your own or by others, gets you noticed not only by the general public but also among the fraternity of journalists. For many writers, being a nationally syndicated columnist is the pot of gold at the end of the rainbow. However, few syndicated columnists get rich on columns alone. Many make their living as newspaper staff columnists; others own businesses or hold down other jobs. The most successful among this elite group also supplement their coffers by

103

writing books, taking on speaking engagements, and making regular media appearances.

Before approaching a syndicate or trying to syndicate a column yourself, determine whether your idea will appeal to a broad national audience. Growing outdoor tropical plants might be a hit in the Sunbelt, but it wouldn't take root in Minnesota or Maine.

Also make sure your idea is one you can keep going for two, three, five years on a national basis. "What people often haven't thought about is how they're going to sustain their column idea," says a Washington Post Writers Group spokesperson. "Make sure you've got a wide enough topic."

Because you'll be facing fierce competition, superlative writing and originality are especially important here. Is your idea unique? Are you just ahead of a trend rather than two steps behind it? Is your style original? Can you do a better job than similar columns already out there? An imitative style or stale idea will never get you into the syndication arena.

Self-Syndication

If you decide to self-syndicate, you will be running a small business. In addition to writing installments one, two, or three times a week, you will have to market the column continually, photocopy and mail it out, keep track of proposals, bill clients, collect fees, and promote the column. With self-syndication comes wider recognition, the increased income of multiple sales, and the independence of working on your own that many self-syndicators feel is, indeed, worth all the effort. Do keep in mind, however, that self-syndication can be a lot of work.

Breaking into self-syndication is easier when you've first placed your column in one newspaper, establishing that as your flagship. Then you have clips to show when approaching other newspaper editors, and they're more apt to take a chance on you, feeling your idea and your ability to deliver reliably have been proven. The more papers you gather in, the more there are that may want to join the club. (If your idea is really hot, you may want to try to place your column with other papers, perhaps after only several installments have appeared in your first publication. Be sure the editor of the first paper knows you're planning to do this.)

In self-syndication, you offer the column to subsequent editors at a lower price than if you were writing for them exclusively. The smaller fee makes your column more attractive—buying it is cheaper for the paper than paying a staff person, stringer, or freelancer to put together copy each week.

THE APPROACH Once again, make the initial contact with editors by mail, sending a cover letter and/or proposal, photocopies of published work, and an SASE if you want your material returned. This cover letter or proposal should also include a list of papers that currently carry the feature.

Market your column to many papers at the same time. However, don't submit simultaneously to publications with overlapping circulation areas. In other words, you can't sell the same column to the *New York Daily News* and the *New York Post*, although you could market the same work to the Newark (N.J.) *Star Ledger* and the *Hartford* (Conn.) *Courant*. When in doubt about whether circulations overlap, check with the newspapers in question.

As we noted in Chapter Five, the *Gale Directory of Publications*, located in the reference section of the library, lists names, addresses, and editors of daily and weekly newspapers in the United States. It's a good idea to call a publication and double-check the name and title of the editor who would buy your type of column. You may be shunted around a little, but verifying this information improves the chances that your letter will reach the correct person.

Lew Sichelman, now a United Feature columnist, talks about his earlier trials as a self-syndicated writer searching for the correct editor to market his real estate feature to. "Once you get past your immediate family [the people you know in the newspaper world], you don't know who to sell your material to. If there's no real estate editor, you may want to try business or features." Sichelman, who worked for years as a newspaper reporter, also says, "A lot of times you don't know who you should be dealing with—the features editor, business editor, real estate editor, managing editor, or advertising vice-president." To avoid all this confusion, pick up the phone.

Once you have the correct editor, make sure your letter is first-rate, says George "Doc"Abraham, who with his wife Katy has been self-syndicating gardening columns for more than forty years. "And don't hurry with the letter," he adds. The Abrahams take turns reading each marketing query to the other, correcting and perfecting as they go along. "We may have to rewrite it as many as five or six times," Abraham says.

The Abrahams, who enjoy the freedom self-syndication offers, have come a long way since the 1940s, when they first began writing. They had just moved to their upstate New York home and bought a commercial florist concern. "Business wasn't good," recounts Katy Abraham. "Doc had always thought about writing a column, so we drove around and talked to the editors of about six little papers. Each of them said 'Send samples.' " The budding writers did and soon their careers as columnists were blossoming. Today the co-authors approach prospective papers by mail, including in their packet a self-addressed, stamped postcard for the editor's reply. The following page shows a sample. When enclosing postcards, type in the name of the editor and paper so when you get the card back, you know who sent it.

Stephen Atlas, on the other hand, has established a successful self-syndicated singles column primarily by using the phone. Atlas, a spontaneous and enthusiastic personality, has found this method works well for him. In each initial pitch he tells what the column is about, why it should appeal to the readership, always mentioning local Parents Without Partners chapters and other singles groups in the area. He follows up by sending a cover letter and samples and then phoning again to get editors' reactions. "I ask their advice," says Atlas. "Editors don't mind giving help, advice, and encouragement. Always be sure to thank them and say you appreciate their encourage-

Dear Doc and Katy Abraham:

☐ Please send us more information _____ yes,
_____ no

☐ Please send us rates

☐ Please send us column

☐ Comments:

        Sincerely,

        Joe Blow, Editor
        Morning Gazette

ment."

Writing texts usually tell writers never to market by phone, but once again we would say at least consider phoning or setting up an in-person interview. When self-syndicating a column, you're acting as a broker, not as a freelancer selling a one-time article. Remember you're competing with syndicates that send sales people around to market their authors. If you do decide to make your move by phone, choose opportune times. "For evening papers," Atlas advises, "don't call until after lunch. For morning papers calling between ten and noon is okay." For weeklies, avoid deadline days, usually the day before the paper comes out.

NEGOTIATIONS With no hard and fast rules about fees to guide them, self-syndicated columnists learn what to ask for by experience. "We charge according to circulation," say the Abrahams. "You have to find out what the columnists get. The weeklies may pay two dollars and the dailies four." Bigger papers pay more—say, from $10 to $20 per installment. You can always ask editors what their rates are, and, after a while, you should have an idea of what a paper will offer based on its circulation. (To learn the circulation of a particular newspaper, look it up in the *Gale Directory of Publications*.)

If an editor is hesitant about running your column, you can resort to the free-sample strategy and let the paper print the feature for a few weeks to gauge reader response. Always offer a specific number of weeks—three, four, five. At the end of that time, call the editor, and if the column has captured an audience, you'll have rung up another sale.

Sell each paper, including the flagship, only first rights in its circulation area, granting them the right to be the first publication in their territory to print the feature. Few papers send contracts, so confirm the details of the agreement (cost, rights being sold, frequency, deadline, word count, subject) in a letter. Most papers and columnists work on a "till forbid" arrangement, meaning that the column will run until one or the other of the parties decides to terminate the relationship.

THE BUSINESS SIDE As you start building a chain of papers, you'll need to devise a bookkeeping system to handle the accounts. A good, functional record-keeping arrangement will ensure the orderly flow of money in and out. It's wise to get professional advice right from the start on setting up books, developing a mechanism for recording payments and disbursements, and sending out bills. Many newspapers mail checks automatically; others must be reminded. Establish a regular billing cycle, requesting payments once a month. Record each fee as it comes in and write down expenses as they occur.

Since all papers won't necessarily buy your column with the same frequency (for example, if you're writing a twice-weekly feature, some publications may want it only once a week), you'll need a system for figuring out what to mail, when, and to whom. You'll also need a mechanism for keeping track of where proposals are and when you plan to follow up. A tickler system, either organized by file cards or noted on a calendar, for example, will clue you in on when it's time to do what. Computer owners may want to invest in software to do all their record- and bookkeeping on their machines.

To Do: Sit down with the *Gale Directory of Publications* and make up a marketing list. Your selections can be arbitrary, choosing newspapers as far-flung as Seattle, Bangor, Miami, and San Diego; just don't overlap circulation areas. On your first run, try to include a mix of dailies and weeklies to broaden your base and also to see if your column appeals more to one than the other.

Pick between twenty-five and fifty to start. Compose a cover letter, using the guidelines in Chapter Five. Then mail your packet to each of the names on the list, sending as many as you can a week. After completing that mailing, do another batch. Keep marketing until you're satisfied with the number of papers carrying your feature (or until you've decided the column isn't selling well enough to pursue marketing it any further).

Meanwhile get record-keeping systems in place to keep track of proposals and expenses. Then get the billing, bookkeeping, and distribution systems organized so you'll be ready to swing into full operation with your first sale.

Syndication

Bombeck. Buchwald. Baker. To become household words like this trio, signing up with a syndicate is the only way to go. But as we've said, while so many strive to reach this pinnacle of success, few make it. King Features, for example, receives more than 200 submissions a week, yet it launches only half a dozen new features a year. The Washington Post Writers Group rejects 99 percent of what they receive, because in the words of one company official, "We are small and prefer to stay that way. We're very selective." From the flood of proposals to United Media's two syndicates, NEA (Newspaper Enterprise Association) and United Feature, only six to eight are chosen each year. Tribune Media Services purchases fewer than a dozen from the thousands of column ideas that come through its doors annually.

Syndicate editors are always on the lookout for a brand-new, fantastic, original idea. However, most of the proposals they buy come from writers with a track record; that is, their columns have appeared in a major newspaper, or the writers have been doing their own syndication or have authored a popular book on a subject that lends itself to a regular newspaper column. Coming up with a super idea and selling to a syndicate right off the bat, although not impossible, is highly unlikely.

In syndication, an agency contracts with an author to write a regular column with a specific number of installments. Then the columnist writes the feature and gives it to the agency, which in turn markets and distributes it to newspapers around the country. For use of the column, a newspaper pays a fee based on its circulation. A small paper might pay $5 weekly for a feature and a large one $20. The syndicate then splits the fee with the writer, usually 50-50, often with production charges (for such things as duplicating and mailing) coming off the top. A select few of the most successful columnists, however, reportedly command 70 percent or more.

In return for its share of the fee, a syndicate performs all the business functions: marketing the work, distributing it, promoting it, sending out bills, and keeping the books. In addition, the agency periodically sends the creator an accounting of where the column has appeared and the money earned. Some syndicates market each person's column individually; others sell several writers' columns as a package, with the subscribing papers free to pick and choose which ones they'll print.

The setup of operations differs from one syndicate to another. In smaller agencies, a few staff people perform all functions, from editing to sales to promotion. Because of their limited personnel, small companies take on small client loads. A columnist won't be lost in a sea of authors here. On the other hand, a larger organization has resources that a littler one doesn't. Personnel is more specialized, with separate staff for sales, editorial functions, and promotion.

Although you give up half the earnings of the column, with this arrangement you'll have more hours for writing and won't get bogged down in the business chores of self-syndication. A syndicate also has expertise and contacts that a self-syndicated entrepreneur would have to take the time to develop. And don't forget, if you sign up with a syndicate, when someone asks what you do, you can toss off, "I'm a syndicated columnist." Oh, the boost to an ego!

THE APPROACH First, note that the syndication process does not require an agent. According to syndicates we talked to, agents won't get a special hearing. "We are as responsive to a creator in Cedar Rapids as to one represented by the Sterling Lord Agency in New York," says James Head, editor of King Features. "Agents take 10 percent of the 50 percent a writer earns. If a creator wants to give away his money, that's up to him. But most of these columnists are working journalists and what do they need an agent for?" So we recommend submitting the column to the syndicates yourself and paying a flat fee to a knowledgeable agent—one well-versed in syndicate contracts—or hiring a lawyer to negotiate your contracts. We'll talk more about contracts later in this chapter.

So how do you choose which syndicates to approach? As with everything in a writer's life, the first step is research. The best source of information is the *Annual Directory of Syndicated Services*, which appears in the final July issue of *Editor & Publisher* magazine for the most recent year (it should be available at your library). In the separate syndicate section, all syndicates are listed along with their addresses, telephone numbers, and key personnel. All current syndicated columns are indexed by author, title, and subject.

Study the subject listings and see which syndicates are already handling your kind of column. Then to make sure you haven't missed any, look through the ads for the syndicates themselves to find their star writers and to get the flavor of each agency. As you read through the directory, identify which syndicates already carry features like yours.

If you're preparing a household hints column similar to Heloise's, you can cross off King Features, which carries her. On the other hand, in fields like political and social commentary, a syndicate like The Washington Post Writers Group, which specializes in opinion, would be a potential market for still another essayist.

Also, be on the lookout for syndicates that do not carry a column like yours but whose offerings your subject might fit in with. For instance, if a syndicate does carry service columns but not one on household hints, as you want to do, then perhaps yours would fit.

Note that philosophies and needs of companies differ. Jake Morrissey, an associate editor at Universal Press Syndicate, points out, "Each syndicate has a specific profile and a specific kind of feature that it carries." "We are known," he explains, "for taking chances and trying new things. We're interested in the kind of readers who grew up during the Vietnam War, are jaded by Watergate, and are interested in how they deal with the world and what their place is in it." The Washington Post Writers Group, on the other hand, focuses on editorial page columnists; puzzles, games, and astrology wouldn't sell here.

How do you find out which syndicates are your best bets? *Writer's Market* profiles syndicates, details needs and submission tips, and names key editors. Many entries also contain information on what a syndicate doesn't want. *How to Make Money in Newspaper Syndication* by Susan Lane also lists syndicates and describes a dozen.

To Do: Make a list of syndicates that fit your needs. Pick the most promising three to five and circle them. They're the ones to pitch first. You can and should approach several at once. Save the list because if you don't succeed initially, you'll want to go on to your second, maybe even third or fourth batch of submissions.

Before approaching a syndicate, send for writer's guidelines, when available. Study, too, the tips for submitting to each syndicate in *Writer's Market*. Your approach to a syndicate should always be by mail, with your letter addressed to a specific person. Again, look up the name of the editor in *Writer's Market* or *Editor & Publisher's Annual Directory of Syndicated Services*. If in doubt about which editor to mail to, choose the ranking or executive editor.

Your proposal should be similar to the type we discussed in Chapter Five, including subject, slant, title, credentials, and statement of audience appeal. In the cover letter do mention simultaneous submission, if that's what you're doing, but do not put a sentence about phoning to follow up. Whether on a proposal or a first follow-up, syndicates do not like to be called.

"The worst mistake that an aspiring columnist can make is trying to do it [marketing a feature] by a telephone call," says James Head, editor of King Features. "There may be exceptions," he continues, "but doing it by phone creates unnecessary problems for the caller and the syndicate in the end. The syndicate is going to want to see the column anyhow [before making a decision]." Diana L. Drake, executive editor at United Media, concurs. "I would much rather get something in writing. People get you on the phone and tell you, 'It will just take a second.' Well, nothing takes a second."

Drake, like all editors, expects cover letters to be clear, concise, and neat. "I frown on typos," she says. "Quite honestly, I like a letter to be perfect. If it's messy, that's not a good sign. If everything's not right, I think, 'This is someone who's going to cost us time and effort in the future.' " Drake does admit that, if an idea is presented messily, but is truly original, her editor's instinct for the unique will get the better of her and she'll give it a read. But why start out with two strikes against you? And why try the patience of anyone you want to sell to?

With your carefully groomed letter include sample columns, either good photocopies (not originals) of those that have appeared in print or neatly typed manuscripts if the column has not been published. Pick a representative selection, six to eight samples of your best work. An editor who likes the column and wants to see more will ask for additional samples. Testimonials—written praise for your column from editors, publishers, and other writers—can be included in the package, but don't overload it. Syndicate editors like to make up their own minds.

Unprofessional submissions—sloppy manuscripts, garish stationery, cutely bound packets, samples of cookies—turn editors off. "I'm not interested in fancy packages," says Michael Argirion, vice president and editor at Tribune Media Services. "Nobody gets dazzled by neon lights."

Don't forget an SASE—one large enough to include all your clips if you want them returned or a #10 business envelope if you don't. When choosing the latter option, indicate your preference in the covering letter.

Expect a four- to eight-week wait. *Writer's Market* listings often give an indication of response time; nevertheless, to be on the safe side, add two or three weeks to that before initiating a follow-up query. A simple letter indicating that you are checking on the status of your proposal will do the trick. State your name, address, phone number, the date you mailed the proposal, and the title and subject of the column. If you don't get a response to this letter within two weeks, then you'd be justified in picking up the phone. But remember, keep the call short and to the point.

PROCESSING THE PROPOSAL What happens once the mail carrier drops a proposal in a syndicate's letter slot? Every agency has its own screening process. At Universal, the submissions are piled on a table in the editorial department. Then each of the five editors picks up proposals as the day's work permits and reads through them. If one shows promise, the editor circulates it among his four colleagues. "We're looking for that rare combination of someone who is able to write well about something and someone who knows a lot about his subject matter and is experienced within his field," states Jake Morrissey. "We're not necessarily looking for a person with a string of degrees. We're looking for a bright, sprightly style of writing." UPS wants a writer who can take a technical and potentially dry subject like computers and make it interesting, he says. Once Morrissey and his fellow editors have found a person who fills the bill and has a subject UPS is in the market for, the lucky writer will get a call.

The not-so-lucky, and that includes the more than 99 percent who don't get a call, receive a response by mail—either a form letter, or if a column idea shows promise, a personal note indicating what the syndicate liked about the feature and encouraging the writer to submit it elsewhere. Occasionally, Universal editors ask an author to resubmit the proposal if it hasn't sold to another syndicate within eight months.

At King Features, manuscripts are reviewed and circulated among the editorial staff, with the more promising proposals landing on the desk of top editor James Head. Only six new columnists a year make it to contract with King. Head, too, encourages an occasional writer to resubmit if King likes the work but is currently booked solid in that particular area. Because there's a turnover in the syndicate world, Head points out, conditions may differ in a year.

Executive editor Tom Reinken of News America Syndicate says, "When proposals come to us, they come to me first. I look at them and if I think they have some merit, I send them to the sales director." Then if the sales director likes a proposal, he forwards it to the sales representative, and if all agree on its worth, the proposal goes to the president of the company for the final review.

When syndicates look for special kinds of columns, they don't work in a vacuum. All along they've been talking to newspaper editors to find out what readers want. NEA, for example, conducts a biannual survey of editors to find out their needs. The Washington Post Writers Group studies a variety of magazines, looking for trends. Staff members at all syndicates read widely, seeking potential columnists for their stable.

HANDLING REJECTION While it's not a good idea to go into something expecting the worst, in this case gird yourself for rejection letters. Even the most talented, creative writer will collect a share of them. "Be ready to be disappointed," says syndicated commentator Roger Simon. "It's a very tough, crowded field. . . . The more narrow the focus of the column idea, the harder the time you will have selling to a syndicate." Therefore, always have a second marketing list and fire off the proposal to the next group of names.

If you're turned down time after time after time, review what you're trying to sell. Is the column well written? Better yet, is it superbly written? If you have any doubts, have someone else evaluate your work. Then go back to a book like Gary Provost's *Make Every Word Count* and see if you're using good writing techniques. Once again, look over the columns of other writers that you admire, then go back and analyze your writing. Does it measure up?

Next, consider whether you're targeting the right syndicates. Have you studied the market and carefully chosen whom to approach? According to James Head of King Features, the biggest error people make is not having done the requisite homework.

If a rejection letter from a syndicate offers comments to improve your column, by all means pay attention. What it says certainly has validity if you want to write for that syndicate and may be just as true if you want to write for others. If you get the same message repeatedly, reconsider your proposal.

If an editor has made suggestions, follow up on them and submit a revised package. If you've received only form rejections but have spent time making significant changes that would affect the marketability of your column, try the proposal another time. "I would want to see a submission again especially if the writer can give me a good reason why I should want to see it," says a Washington Post Writers Group official. In other words, don't give up after the first try. (When you send amended copy, mention in the cover letter that this is a revision, and note if you've adopted changes the editor recommended.)

When an idea is rejected but you know it's a winner, consider self-syndication. Maybe your feature will get picked up by a syndicate after you've been successful at selling it yourself. Real estate columnist Lew Sichelman, for example, had built up his own self-syndication business to about 100 papers when United Feature called him with an offer.

No matter what, keep on writing. Many local columnists are grabbed up by a syndicate that has seen them in print. Erma Bombeck and George Plagenz were plucked from the pages of their area newspapers and Dr. Michael Fox from the pages of *McCall's* by savvy syndicates.

ACCEPTANCE AND NEGOTIATION Suppose you hit the jackpot and a syndicate says, "We're interested." What happens next? The syndicate will call to iron out details and possibly request more samples. Once you've reached an agreement and the column has been approved, it's time to begin contract negotiations.

Before starting talks with a syndicate, it's a good idea to consult a lawyer, preferably one versed in publishing contracts, or an agent willing to work on a flat-fee basis to negotiate the contract. A knowledgeable third party whose ego is not involved in the creation of your work can negotiate unemotionally for you and probably get you better terms.

Remember, you are entering a buyers' market. Thousands of people are competing for a few slots, and your leverage in negotiation will be limited, depending on your experience and the desirability of your idea.

Jeffrey L. Squires, an attorney practicing law in Washington, D.C., points out that the outcome of every issue that arises in syndicate contract negotiations hinges on bargaining power. "Ann Landers has bargaining power that Joe Blow doesn't have. Say Joe Blow goes to one of the syndicates and says, 'I've got a great idea for a column,' and they say, 'Terrific, we'll negotiate with you.' He's going to have to take the deal they offer." Squires also says, "Another thing that's involved in negotiation is the art of persuasion and he [the columnist] may not be trained in or very good at that."

However, the attorney continues, the situation can be changed with good representation, whether it be a lawyer or a knowledgeable agent. He points out that Joe Blow would be better off "with somebody [a lawyer] sitting down and trying to explain to the syndicate why it's in the syndicator's interest to do what's in Joe Blow's interest, why it will serve the syndicator's profit-motivated purpose to treat Joe Blow well—to give him more literary freedom, to give him more control over the content of his column, to offer him inducement to perform in a fashion that will increase the attractiveness of the column to potential purchasers."

Standard syndicate contracts call for a 50-50 split of earnings, although hot properties may wangle a higher percentage. Some syndicates include a provision in the contract for deducting production expenses from the gross before splitting earnings with the writer. When this is the case, many authors try to have a cap on production expenses written into the agreement. Other syndicate contracts offer creators a straight fee, buying the column outright for a specified amount.

Other points you might want to negotiate or have your lawyer or agent negotiate for you are:

- The right to a periodic reporting of papers subscribing to your column, of fees collected, and of expenses incurred.
- The right to audit your accounts at the syndicate.
- The right to request an accounting of the number of sales calls made for your column.
- Copyright ownership, including what rights a syndicate purchases. If you give up copyright ownership, will it be for the length of the contract or in perpetuity? Will you get a fair percentage on subsidiary rights?
- Control over editorial content. Will the editor consult you if he or she wants to alter a particular installment? Many syndicates say they run changes past a writer as a matter of course, but you may still want to have this agreement in print.
- Promotion, what a syndicate will do to promote your feature. How much advertising will it do and in what media? From what monies will advertising costs be paid—the syndicate's, the columnist's, or jointly?
- Minimum money guarantee. A guarantee of a certain base income can be written into the contract ensuring that earnings can't dip below a specified figure.
- Duration of contract. Most contracts run from one to five years.
- Automatic renewal clause, a clause that extends your contract at the same level of services and remuneration for the renewal period. A predetermined performance level for the syndicate and/or a clause that allows both parties to renegotiate the contract can be written in.
- Right to sell other work. Most writers try to retain the right to sell their subsequent creations to whomever they choose; however, many grant their syndicates a first look at future output.
- Commitment by the syndicate to sell the column to at least a minimum number of newspapers or daily newspapers.
- Indemnification or libel protection. Can you be included in the syndicate's umbrella policy or will you need coverage of your own? Who will bear the cost of any libel suits against you? Will you and the syndicate split them?
- Survivors' clause that channels your earnings to your estate should you die.

Before signing your name on the line, check out "A How-to Guide for Getting Syndicated" in *Editor & Publisher*'s August 31, 1985, issue or its partial reprint in the magazine's 1986 *Annual Directory of Syndicated Services* and look at *How to Make Money in Newspaper Syndication* by Susan Lane.

AFTER THE CONTRACT Before your column makes its national debut, you and the syndicate, jointly and separately, will have to do a good amount of labor. Promotion must be worked up— sales kits, brochures, and other materials—the column itself must be written and refined, sales pitches must be delivered, and agreements must be closed. This could take anywhere from two months to an entire year.

Once your column is in production, you may be working four to five weeks in advance or, in the case of timely editorial features, only a day or two ahead. Columnists who write the latter usually transmit by modem, computer to computer. Less timely columns are often mailed into syndicates in batches.

CONCLUSION

Your column's a success. You're beginning to develop a following. Letters and phone calls are starting to come in. Readers agree with you. They disagree. They ask your advice. They have advice for you. They need more information. They give you information. They tell you stories. They pour out their souls. Each installment of your column will generate its own response.

When it comes to fans, expect the unexpected. Columns that writers expect to draw an overwhelming response often fizzle out, while others on seemingly more pedestrian topics launch an avalanche of mail and a chorus of ringing telephones. And often writers say they can't figure out in advance which will bring what.

Roger Simon remembers writing a column a few years back about a woman who won a beauty contest at the 1933-

34 World's Fair in Chicago—Miss Television of 1934 (yes, there was television back then, he assures us). He tells of going to her tiny apartment crammed with memorabilia. The door opened and he found himself greeted by an old woman bedecked in a ball gown and crowned with a tiara. Touched by the aged beauty queen and the importance of that ancient title in her life, he went back to his office and wrote about her in what he thought was a moving column that would generate many empathetic letters. Instead, he got, in his own words, "Nothing. Zip. Not one comment." Then in 1986, he once again spotlighted her. "I wrote a little retrospective piece on her," he says. This time he didn't anticipate much response. Once again the public fooled him. "People stopped me. They called me. They wrote letters." With a pause for appreciation of the irony, he adds, "Go figure it."

Isaac Rehert, whose *Sun* columns talked about life on the farm, recalls a piece he wrote about the day he realized there were too many roosters in his hen house and how he planned to control the population by turning roosters into roasters. Almost before he could lift a forkful of poultry to his lips, the phone rang.

"I always thought you were such a sensitive, caring person," cried the indignant reader. "How could you do it?"

"Do what?" Rehert wanted to know.

"Eat your own roosters."

Patiently he explained that all the roosters wanted to do the whole day long was practice their procreative technique, exhausting a lot of hens. One rooster, he went on patiently, is all a coopful of hens needs.

"Then," she declared, obviously lighting upon the solution, "don't have any roosters."

"Well," Rehert pointed out. "We need roosters. You can't have chickens without them."

Thoughtful silence. Then, "But don't chickens come from eggs?"

Once again, Rehert, who never imagined he'd be in the position of giving a correspondence course in sex education, explained that eggs must be fertilized.

The caller was surprised.

As she hung up, the writer chuckled to himself thinking. *"Readers will be readers and that's exactly why I write my column, to teach city bumpkins that chickens do indeed come from eggs."*

If you write a service column, your readers will continually surprise you with the kinds of information they ask for. Take, for instance, the phone call Atlanta weather columnist Charles Salter received one March from an area travel agent. "Can you please tell me the time of sunset on May 25 in Key West, Florida?"

Taken aback, the columnist asked why.

"Oh," the caller explained, "one of my clients wants to have a sunset cocktail party there that day."

Curiosity satisfied, Salter supplied her with the exact hour and minute.

One of the most unusual stories of reader response was reported by Bonnie J. Schupp in her "Camera Bag" column in *The Evening Sun*; she received a postcard from Ghana asking for information on cameras. Intrigued, Schupp replied, saying she didn't sell photographic equipment, and asked how the correspondent had gotten hold of her column. Her correspondent wrote back that he had found a scrap of a foreign newspaper on the ground on a sparsely traveled road near his African home. It was Schupp's column. The man had always been fascinated by cameras, but since he earned only a dollar a day, he'd never been able to buy one. Somehow he hoped through writing to her he would be able to realize his dream.

Dee Hardie finds that her homespun musings sometimes bring more than letters. In one case, it brought teapots. She had written a column for *House Beautiful* telling of her lifelong passion for collecting the brewing vessels and describing teatime at her house. In response, readers rushed to the post office to mail her packets of their favorite brews. Others sent teacups. One 85-year-old woman tenderly took her prized blue and white china pot from her kitchen shelf, wrapped it carefully, and posted it to Hardie, since the woman had no child to will it to.

Environmental columnist Gordon Bishop has discovered that people really do believe in what he's writing. After a column advocating free access to New Jersey's beaches, fans of the Newark *Star-Ledger* columnist ripped his piece from the paper, took it to the shore, and waved it in the faces of the people collecting fees at entrance gates to the sandy strips.

Religion columnist George Plagenz, when he was writing his rate-the-churches column in Cleveland, gave one house of worship ten stars out of twelve, an unusually high score. The next Sunday the sign outside the church, which usually announced the sermon, instead proclaimed, "Cove Methodist Church—Approved by God and Plagenz."

Another church that he evaluated earned only one star out of a possible three for friendliness. Instead of calling to berate him as members of other poorly rated houses of worship had done, this congregation called for help. The members asked Plagenz to come and speak to their greeters. He did, and from that time forward, all newcomers were heartily welcomed by fellow worshippers as they stepped into the church's lobby.

> *"You can't allow yourself to get a swelled head. You quickly realize that not everybody knows your name, especially when you're trying to cash a check. All of us are putting out a product. If you remember your job isn't to make yourself a celebrity but to explain all this [your column subject] to your readers, you'll do a lot better."—Barry Garron, Kansas City* Star *TV and radio critic.*

While getting readers to react to your words is rewarding, don't expect to change the world every time out. As Roger Simon notes, "Remember that your job is to communicate and tell a story. It's nice to do good, but that is frosting on the cake." Back in 1981, Simon wrote a column that explored major flaws in security at Chicago's O'Hare Airport. About five years later, the television show *60 Minutes* did the same story, which showed Simon just how influential his story had been— half a decade later the airport still had the same security problems.

How do columnists handle the response they generate? Do they read every letter and do they reply to them all? What about phone calls? Do they make themselves available to answer every ring? What about disgruntled readers? How do they handle them?

Some top writers like Heloise and Ann Landers have a staff to help them wade through the piles of questions, information, and opinions they receive from readers. Other columnists read and answer the mail themselves. *Colonial Homes*'s Dorothy Hammond gives personal replies to questions she can't fit into her antiques column. "A lot of my mail is from small towns and rural areas where people don't have access to information," she explains. So whenever she can, she picks up the telephone. By calling, she avoids getting into a time-consuming pen pal correspondence. True, she runs up her phone bill, but she can devote the time she saves to the small publications firm she runs.

Doc and Katy Abraham, who invite queries in their various gardening columns, have been inundated by as many as 1,000 letters a week. To deal with their pleasant dilemma, when their children were small, they conscripted them into a nightly mail sorting bee. Later when an aunt came to live with them, they sat her down with the stacks. The resourceful couple has even invited friends for a spaghetti dinner at their house, offering an extra course—mail sorting. After the sorting, the Abrahams choose which letters they'll answer in their columns and earmark the rest for personal replies.

In addition, from time to time, the Abrahams gather some of their more complimentary fan letters and send them off to their editors to let them know that their readers like what they see. "When we get a letter saying, 'We enjoy your column in the *Gazette*,'" explains Doc Abraham, "we draw a circle around *Gazette* and mail it to the editor." Many times readers, grateful for personal answers to their questions, ask "Is there anything I can do for you?" "Sure," reply the Abrahams. "Write and tell your editor you like our service." This self-promotion can only pay dividends.

George Plagenz answers all his correspondents, too—except the vitriolic ones. Other columnists, in the interest of economy, reply only to letters that contain self-addressed, stamped envelopes. Still others admit they don't answer fan mail, preferring to direct their energies into writing columns.

Like so many other columnists, pharmaceutical writer Joe Graedon includes a disclaimer on the bottom of every install-ment of his feature, stating that he cannot answer every ques-tion. But this doesn't mean he doesn't want to help his readers. There just isn't time to reply to the many queries he gets each day—some of which could take a half hour or more to answer properly. "The real guilt trip," he confides, "is the volume of mail that we can't answer personally." But when people ask life-and-death questions, Graedon picks up the phone.

As for telephone calls, some writers, particularly newspaper staffers like Richard Cohen and Roger Simon, can be reached just by dialing their newspaper offices. These writers take time out of their schedules to listen to their readers.

To avoid having their workday eaten up by fanatical fans, many columnists employ answering services or machines to screen messages. Well-paid columnists like Art Buchwald have staffs to perform these functions. Some of the bigger-name writers may also have unlisted home and, even, office phone numbers to discourage overzealous admirers and cranks, and to preserve privacy. Naturally, having an unlisted business number wouldn't work for community columnists and those who want a maximum amount of feedback from their reader-ship, but it does for writers who want to discourage drop-in visitors and casual callers and to maintain a "fence" around their private lives.

But even within that fence there will be people who pester you at parties, friends of friends who call for advice when you're on a tight deadline, and strangers who accost you as you're digging into a birthday dinner of lobster thermidor at the Top of the Price List restaurant. You'll quickly learn about typesetting errors, grammatical mistakes, and weak ideas you've had in your column. It's as if everyone from vacuum cleaner salespeople to tree surgeons to orthodontists knows how to write your column better than you do and will be hap-py to tell you. Be forewarned and be prepared.

Overly ardent fans will also overstep the bounds of the columnist-reader relationship by asking for favors. For exam-ple, Art Buchwald drolly reports that 80 percent of his fan mail is from people who think he's an employment agency, or should be. "Can you get me a job?" they write. "The rest are kids who want me to do their term papers," the columnist adds with his customary dry humor. "And they want it done by Thursday."

Recognition, especially if you have your photo in the paper, comes with the territory, and it never hurts your reputation to be polite to even the most obnoxious character. However, you would do well to perfect the art of cutting off conversations quickly but graciously and letting out-of-line comments slide over you. A few readers may test your patience now and then, but most are just what you hoped you'd find—an appreciative audience that looks forward to your byline.

In this book, we've given you the basics of how to write and sell your column. We wish you luck and hope that the next time we meet, we will be reading your words just as you have read ours.

APPENDIX

Legal Concerns

Below is a very brief summary of items of legal concern to columnists. We have included these to make you aware of them and to give you an overview. But a book like this can't hope to treat these subjects in depth. For more detailed information, consult legal guides on the subject (see the bibliography for some references) and/or a lawyer familiar with publishing.

Copyright. Think of each column as a piece of property that you, the creator, have the right to rent or sell. The property is the tangible work itself, the order in which you've placed the words on the paper, not the idea. (Ideas, titles, facts, short phrases, slogans are not copyrightable.) Copyright is a form of ownership protection given under federal law to an original work. Under the law, from the work's inception, you as creator have the right to do or authorize the following:

- to reproduce the copyrighted work in copies
- to prepare derivative works based upon the copyrighted work
- to distribute copies of the copyrighted work to the public by sale or other transfer of ownership, or by rental, lease, or lending
- to display the copyrighted work publicly
- to perform the copyrighted work publicly

Under federal law, as soon as you create a work, it is automatically copyrighted. You can also officially register your column or a group of your columns with the Copyright Office at The Library of Congress. This provides you with a certificate of proof of ownership should you ever have to go to court. (You can write to The Copyright Office, Library of Congress, Washington DC 20559 for a packet of information explaining the law and containing registration forms.) Another way you can protect your ownership is by placing the copyright symbol © 19-- and your name on each manuscript. This is necessary if your column is to be printed in a publication that is itself copyrighted but you want to retain copyright ownership. This is also necessary to protect your ownership if you submit your work to a publication that is not copyrighted. In both cases you must request that the editor print the notice on your column.

As creator, you can sell the copyright—for example, giving the property and all the attendant privileges outright to a publication or a syndicate. Or you can transfer the use of this property for a limited time or purpose (that is, to print once or to reprint) by selling certain rights. Selling first serial rights, for instance, means the publication has the authority to be the first to print your column. Then you are free to sell that particular installment of your feature someplace else. Selling all rights means you give up all rights to use or sell the work in its present form anywhere else.

An alternative is to offer first serial rights in a publication's circulation area, a necessity for self-syndicators. Self-syndicators should always confirm they are selling first rights in that publication's circulation area in each agreement letter.

When your work is copyrighted, no one may reproduce it without your permission. To do so is infringement. However, someone may quote from your column without your permission, provided they stay within fair use guidelines and give you credit. That means a small portion of the work can be quoted for educational, research, news, or critical purposes. But because the guidelines are hazy, if you're quoting from someone else's work and are in doubt about how much you can use, ask the author's permission.

Libel. "Libel," says attorney Jeffrey L. Squires, "is anything written that is false and injures another person." Libel can occur even if the injured party isn't named but can be identified from details or descriptions in your column. For a libel case to stand up in court, it must be proven that what you've written is untrue, Squires points out. "Truth," he explains, "is a total defense to libel. Successfully defending a libel claim by establishing truthfulness, however, is not always the easiest thing in the world.

"The technical principles governing libel are, of course,

very complex," Squires continues. "For example, some people have heard of the principle of the *New York Times vs. Sullivan* case, which requires that people who are 'public figures' prove not only that they were libeled, but that the false statements made against them were made with 'malice' as defined by law—with knowledge or reckless carelessness."

Libel suits can drain money, energy, and health, so be sure of your facts and be prepared for any possible negative repercussions if you go ahead and write a controversial column. Editors, too, are concerned with libel and for a questionable piece may request their legal department to go over the column too—but don't count on it.

Jack Anderson's investigative columns are meticulously checked out by his staff reporters, editors, lawyers, and then by United Feature's staff. Yet even with all the reviewing, Anderson's organization still gets hit occasionally by people who allege they've been libeled. As of this writing, according to his associate Joseph Spear, the organization has won all the suits, but it's been time-consuming and expensive.

Check with a lawyer before you pen a potentially libelous column. The law on libel is quite complex and an attorney can advise you on the intricacies of what you're dealing with. Investigative columnists and others whose work borders on the controversial would also do well to read extensively on this subject.

Fair comment. Under the law, writers may express opinions or voice criticism in columns, reviews, and other written forms, provided the writer presents the work as opinion, not fact; does not maliciously defame someone; and bases his or her opinion on fact. This permits a writer, for example, to review a book and say the characters are cardboard and the plot is weak.

Invasion of privacy. "Linked with libel," says Squires, "is something called invasion of privacy to which truth is not a complete defense. Invasion of privacy is undue intrusiveness into one's private affairs." Invasion of privacy can be actionable if you've written a column that discloses facts about a private individual's personal life that are offensive to community standards and not of legitimate concern to the public. However, people in the public eye, like actors and politicians, or people caught up in current public events, lose some of their right to privacy because they are newsworthy. But remember, the line is a blurry one, and when in doubt, check with a lawyer.

BIBLIOGRAPHY

GENERAL

Burack, Sylvia K., ed. *The Writer's Handbook.* Boston: The Writer, Inc. Use current edition. Contains articles covering wide range of subjects of interest to writers. "Getting Started in Book Reviewing" by Lynne Sharon Schwartz is recommended for those interested in the field.

Evans, Glen, ed. *The Complete Guide to Writing Nonfiction.* Cincinnati: Writer's Digest Books, 1983. Advice from pros in all fields of writing crammed into 870 information-packed pages.

Gale Directory of Publications. Detroit, MI: Gale Research Co. Use current year. Lists editor/publisher, circulation, frequency of publication, address, telephone number of newspapers and magazines in the United States and Canada. Also contains a separate listing of feature editors of bigger newspapers and subject listings of publications.

Knott, Leonard. *Writing After Fifty.* Cincinnati: Writer's Digest Books, 1985. For those who've retired from one career and want to begin another as a writer. A good discussion on reviewers vs. critics for would-be movie, theatre, and book columnists.

Literary Marketplace: The Directory of American Book Publishing. New York: R. R. Bowker Company. Use current edition. Lists news services and syndicates with a capsule profile of some. Also lists major newspapers and their book review editors, book publishers, writers' conferences and associations, some columnists, and other categories pertaining to book publishing industry.

Mack, Karin, and Eric Skjei. *Overcoming Writing Blocks.* Los Angeles: J. P. Tarcher, Inc., 1979. For anyone who has ever been stopped by writer's block or may be in the future.

Polking, Kirk, ed. *Freelance Jobs for Writers.* Cincinnati: Writer's Digest Books, 1984. See "Column Writing" by Al Eason for one self-syndicated columnist's advice.

Writer's Market. Cincinnati: Writer's Digest Books. Use latest edition. An annual marketing guide for writers, containing 4,000 markets—magazines, newspapers, book and script publishers. Articles in front and back sections give business information and tips.

Zobel, Louise Purwin. *The Travel Writer's Handbook.* Cincinnati: Writer's Digest Books, 1984. Details the ins and outs of travel writing, including an excellent section about making your adventures come alive on the page.

WRITING STYLE, TECHNIQUES, AND GRAMMAR

Hall, Donald. *Writing Well.* Boston: Little, Brown and Company, 1985. A good general guide for anyone who writes or uses the English language.

Pinckert, Robert C. *Pinckert's Practical Grammar.* Cincinnati: Writer's Digest Books, 1986. A lively, practical guide to usage, punctuation, and style.

Provost, Gary. *Make Every Word Count.* Cincinnati: Writer's Digest Books, 1980. An absolute must for every writer. For learning how to develop a style and to make words work for you, this book is the best.

Ross-Larson, Bruce. *Edit Yourself: A Manual for Everyone Who Works with Words.* New York: W. W. Norton & Company, 1982. An easy-to-use manual to trim the fat from your writing.

Ruehlmann, William. *Stalking the Feature Story.* Cincinnati: Writer's Digest Books, 1978. Columnists, too, will capture a wealth of information on writing style and story development.

INTERVIEWING AND RESEARCH

Brady, John. *The Craft of Interviewing.* New York: Random House, 1979. Getting people to agree to interviews and what to do with them when you've got them.

Clark, Bernadine, ed. *The Writer's Resource Guide.* Cincinnati: Writer's Digest Books, 1983. An encyclopedia of organizations, companies, and special interest groups that could keep a writer intrigued for years. A good source of ideas and where to go for information.

Horowitz, Lois. *Knowing Where to Look: The Ultimate Guide to Research.* Cincinnati: Writer's Digest Books, 1984. Whether it's a quotation, statistic, biographical fact, study, address, or expert you need, this book will steer you in the right direction.

Miller, Mara. *Where to Go for What.* Englewood Cliffs, N.J.: Prentice Hall, Inc., 1981. Where to look to find information and how to use resources ranging from telephone directories to think-tanks to dissertation abstracts.

BUSINESS OF BEING A WRITER, LEGAL CONCERNS

Beil, Norman, ed. *The Writer's Legal and Business Guide to Motion Pictures, Television, & Book Publishing.* New York: Arco Publishing, Inc., 1984. Detailed sections on copyright and legal liability.

Cassill, Kay. *The Complete Handbook for Freelance Writers.* Cincinnati: Writer's Digest Books, 1981. Discusses record keeping, bookkeeping, contracts, promotion, sales, and many other facets of the writing business.

Crawford, Tad. *The Writer's Legal Guide.* New York: Hawthorn Books, Inc., 1979. Contracts, copyright, income tax, vanity publishing—it's all here.

Hanson, Nancy E. *How You Can Make $20,000 a Year Writing No Matter Where You Live.* Cincinnati: Writer's Digest Books, 1980. Practical suggestions for increasing your writing income. What other jobs you can take on to support your column habit.

Lant, Jeffrey L. *The Unabashed Self-Promoter's Guide.* Cambridge: JLA Publications, 1983. For anyone who wants to get the most out of a publicity campaign. Tips on putting together a media kit, getting media attention, and presenting yourself effectively.

Polking, Kirk, and Rose Adkins. *Beginning Writer's Answer Book*. 2nd ed. Cincinnati: Writer's Digest Books, 1984. Helpful tidbits on column writing, rights, legal concerns, and markets, interspersed among nuggets of information of interest to all writers.

Polking, Kirk, and Leonard S. Meranus, ed. *Law & the Writer.* 3rd ed. revised, Cincinnati: Writer's Digest Books, 1985. Covers contracts, copyright, libel, plagiarism, obscenity, taxes, social security, and syndication contracts.

OF SPECIAL INTEREST TO COLUMNISTS

Grauer, Neil A. *Wits & Sages.* Baltimore: The Johns Hopkins University Press, 1984. A discussion of twelve of America's best-known columnists and their work. Recommended reading for those interested in doing political and social commentary.

Lane, Susan. *How to Make Money in Newspaper Syndication.* Irvine: Newspaper Syndication Specialists, 1985. A book offering information you can't find anywhere else. Prospective columnists and cartoonists would do well to look through this volume.

Weiner, Richard. *Syndicated Columnists.* New York: Public Relations Publishing Co., Inc. 1979. Contains a history of column writing and listing of columnists. Check 1982 edition called *Syndicated Columnists Directory* for updated section on columnists.

INDEX